STAR TEAM^{SM}
DYNAMICS

12 LESSONS LEARNED FROM EXPERIENCED TEAM BUILDERS

JANELLE BRITTAIN, MBA, CSP

The Chicago Mercantile Exchange History of Innovation TimeLine was reprinted in part with the permission of the Chicago Mercantile Exchange. Taken from the CME website, http://www.cme.com/exchange/history.html.

Excerpts from *1001 Ways to Reward Employees* by Bob Nelson (Workman Publishing Company), Copyright © 1997 by Bob Nelson: http://www.nelson-motivation.com. Reprinted by permission of the author. All rights reserved.

Interior illustrations by Gary Frontier of Graphite Images   6/00
Cover design by Michael Komarck and Craig Hines

© 1999 by Janelle Brittain

This publication is designed to provide accurate and authoritative information in regard to the subject matter covered. It is sold with the understanding that the publisher is not engaged in rendering legal, accounting, or other professional service. If legal advice or other expert assistance is required, the services of a competent professional person should be sought. *From a Declaration of Principles jointly adopted by a committee of the American Bar Association and a committee of Publishers.*

10 9 8 7 6 5 4 3 2 1

Library of Congress Cataloging in Publication Data

Brittain, Janelle, 1949–
    Star team dynamics : 12 lessons learned from experienced team builders / by Janelle Brittain.
        p.   cm.
    Includes bibliographical references and index.
    ISBN 1-886939-28-4
    1. Teams in the workplace   I. Title.
HD66.B755   1998
658.4'02--dc21   98-33952
                                                             CIP

Oakhill Press
3400 Willow Grove Court
Greensboro, NC 27410-8600
Printed in the United States of America

Contents

Stage 1:
The Decision To Launch Into A Team-Based Culture

Stage II:
Planning And Designing A Star Team Culture

Stage III:
Implementing And Maintaining Star Teams

Contents

Acknowledgments

My passion for helping organizations avoid the pain experienced by the pioneers in their transition into teams is what led me to write this book. The challenges that caused many companies to want to toss their entire team experiment out the window were, to me, a valuable learning experience. I am grateful to the following individuals and organizations who share my belief in teams, and who carry the same zest for learning and the torch of hope for the future.

When Linkage Incorporated ventured out in 1997 to hold its first national conference on the subject of "The Best of Teams," its visionary leaders were steadfastly devoted to creating an open learning environment that many team builders had not seen before. They helped link me up with companies of various sizes and types of team building experience. From their 1997 and 1998 conference attendees, I was able to glean many wonderful "lessons learned" to pass on to others.

Thanks also to the numerous unnamed organizations who shared their pain, but preferred not to be quoted. It may be of interest to the reader that these companies are still using teams and continue to learn from their trial and error.

One person who was a constant encourager, advisor, and "detail queen" and who constantly irritated and delighted me, was Diane Valletta, the editor of the book. Without her this book could never have come to fruition. She has an uncanny ability to make the words sing, while simultaneously policing countless details of grammar, spelling, syntax and consistency. Her devotion to this project often saw her working through the night until the sunrise, to meet our ambitious deadlines.

My Program Management team at the Dynamic Performance Institute, Mary Wallace and Marilyn Anderson, were the backbone of this project. Mary's encouragement and control of the office allowed me to focus on the book during hectic times. Her sense of organization and speedy fingers helped render on paper the massive volume of background material I had collected through the research stage. Marilyn was amazing, bringing a focus and dedication to sit for hours inputting edits as the project neared completion, and applying her computer wizardry to formats and headings.

Few were aware of my silent co-author — Alex the cat. Whenever I sat down to write — no matter what the time of day — she would suddenly appear, bringing the writing muse with her. She always knew which were the most important papers and showed them to me by sleeping on them.

Writing was often impossible when business became too hectic at DPI headquarters. Two friends graciously offered me their beautiful and inspirational home in the Wisconsin woods to get away to write. Many thanks to Jan Schmidt and Jan Terry.

Despite extreme time pressures, several colleagues gave of their time and intellect to read the manuscript and offer advice. Special thanks to Ed Oakley, Randi Killian, Jan Schrader and Joyce Gioia.

Oakhill Press has been wonderful to work with. Thanks to Roger Herman and Joyce Gioia, who have been exuberant mentors and supporters and to Paula Gould who has been our General in charge of the production process.

Dr. Terry Paulson was kind enough to offer his thoughts in the foreword. In addition to being an accomplished author, speaker, and consultant, this remarkable and witty man is also president of the National Speakers Association, an international organization dedicated to advancing the art and value of experts who speak professionally. On a personal note, the education and support I have received from this wonderful organization have been extremely helpful in advancing my career.

Finally, thanks to our many clients over many years, who though widely varied in industry, size, location and challenges, are united in their openness to bringing us onto their team, as we are all in the search for stellar performance.

Janelle Brittain, MBA, CSP

Foreword

e all know that teams are critical and that no one leader can ever have all the information or insight to discern the right answer for every problem. As one sign at Motorola says so eloquently, "We believe in collaborative problem solving. In school that is called cheating." It might as well be cheating for how poorly most organizations prepare their leaders and associates to effectively use and participate in teams.

I have heard a common question repeated many times over the last few years: "I know I need teams, but how do you get them to work?" Everyone knows they need teams, but for the life of them, they have had trouble making them work.

If you are one of those leaders who has wanted a practical resource with real-life tools to help any organization create great team, help has arrived in the form of *Star Team Dynamics: 12 Lessons Learned from Experienced Team Builders.* This is a long overdue collection of lessons learned in a decade of reviewing best practices and research on how to make teams work.

Janelle cuts to the heart of the issues and processes involved in making teams deliver for the organizations and for the individuals involved. It's an honest book. It faces the fact that you need high functioning individuals trained and committed to making teams produce results. That means individuals must be helped to develop the skills that add value to the strategic goal of the team. They have to know how to communicate so people listen. They need to know how to listen so collaborative synergy can bear fruit. Teams must also be held accountable.

This is one book that doesn't stop with theory and dry strategies. This book addresses the tricky interpersonal problems that rear their ugly head every time teams are formed. Let's face it. The only places where perfect people or teams exist are in educational movies and management training books. This is no "Pollyanna Piece." This book struggles with the real life problems. Learn when to take people off teams and how to deal with it when you must. Learn how leaders can sabotage otherwise high-functioning teams. Learn when teams aren't the right choice. After all, why talk about theory alone, when you need the nuts and bolts guidance to handle the people problems that always occur when people work together to change organizational cultures.

This book is practical and structured to help you get to the information you need when you need it. You'll learn about the choice to team and what kind of team to use. You'll learn how to plan the launch and how to manage the care and feeding of mature teams. You will want to review the lessons learned over and over again, and the book is designed to help you find the lessons you need, whether you are just starting or trying to retool teams that are already formed and working.

There are now perpetual teams that start work in San Francisco only to ship their work to Korea and then on to Latvia or Bombay before returning in the morning to San Francisco in a never-ending series of handoffs. This book will keep up with the pace of change in this chaotic and dispersed global economy. You'll learn how to make virtual teams produce and how to use the speed and the collaborative tools shaped for the Internet. With the speed of change today comes real life stories of successes and failures. This book has the guts to look at both.

In short, this is one book that won't sit on your shelf. Once you start reading, it won't be long before you're saying to yourself: "Oh, that's why that didn't work!" or "That's just the insight I needed!" The greatest gift a book provides is the changes it generates even months after reading. Keep a pad of paper and a pencil at the ready. When you read this book, you will find many changes worth doing something about. In fact, with Janelle Brittain's book, making teams work just got a little bit easier. Here's some advice: Put a star team in your organization's constellation.

Terry L. Paulson, PhD, CSP, CPAE
Author of *They Shoot Managers, Don't They?*
1998/99 President of the National Speakers Association

Introduction

*P*roducing more with less is a motivating force which in the 1990's has catapulted teams into the corporate culture as a "ready solution." Most companies who jumped on the teams bandwagon expected immediate transformation and results. For many, frustration set in early. Employees rebelled. Conflicts ensued. Teams crashed and burned. After listening to endless stories of struggle and angst from people in these organizations, I found one day I could no longer stand by — I had to do something more to help.

As an observer, I saw a trend emerging. It became clear to me that most of these companies were focused on the *process* of developing the team — not on helping the *people* transition and grow into their new roles. While anointing the employees as teams, management often did not change their own roles or the way they manage. This oversight undercut the success of the teams. As a result, many teams and companies became disillusioned with the teams approach in the 1990's.

This is unfortunate, because a carefully organized, carefully implemented team-based culture is an exceptional solution for the evolution of the third millennium companies who plan to outperform their competition and thrive amidst fast changing environs. So instead of viewing the 1990's struggles with teams as proof that teams won't work, I choose to view the period as a time of trial and error where many important lessons have been learned.

It is from this perspective that I was motivated to create a book based on the lessons learned from team building attempts in the 1990's. After interviewing many companies across North America, researching many other studies and writings, adding my own nearly ten years of helping 1990's teams grow, and much reflection, I have developed the 12 Lessons presented in these pages.

Star Team Dynamics, the foundation of the book, is my own vision for how successful organizations will operate in the future. As described in the next chapter, Star Team Dynamics refers to people relating to one another based on a star shaped model instead of the old triangle/pyramid model. The beauty of the star model is that it stimulates interaction, communication and thinking . . . important skills to enter into the Knowledge Age.

How to get the most out of this book

This book is both a step-by-step guide and a reference manual. Once you've read it, you will probably want to keep it handy to pull out when you are establishing a new team or facing some challenge. Most books on team building in the 1990's have done a good job of discussing the theory behind teams and some process on establishing them. This book does some of that, but goes an important step further. We address the tough, sticky issues — the dynamics of the people. We go to the very core of management's and staff's real thinking and motivation. And we share both the successes and failures of real life companies and organizations, to help you quickly see the application of the lessons.

This book addresses three stages of team culture development:

Stage I: The Decision to Launch into a Team-Based Culture (Prologue and Lesson #1)

Stage II: Planning and Designing a Star Team Culture (Lessons #2–6)

Stage III: Implementing and Maintaining Star Teams (Lessons #7–12)

The first two chapters lay the groundwork for deciding whether teams make sense in your organization or situation. They are the theory and the overall strategy. Your feasibility team will want to be sure to read these chapters.

After the decision is made to ascend to a team based culture, the planning team will find Lessons #2 through 6 critical for designing the plan and the transition. Lessons #7 through 12 are for everyone who is on a team. Here readers will learn about the vital ground rules and relationship building that are necessary to create a supportive, exceptionally performing Star Team. As time goes on and new teams are being established, you may want to pull the book down off the shelf once again to review Lessons #3, 7, 8, 9 and 12. When you are experiencing the tougher people challenges, you'll find useful information in Lessons #10 and 11.

MATURE TEAMS

Mature teams who are struggling will want to carefully read Lessons #2–12 in order to pinpoint what detail, process or people focus was missed. Mature teams will find this book a useful diagnostic tool to help with specific challenges. Often the result of faulty team set-up is not seen until after the team has been underway for six months or more. Compare your set-up with the suggestions offered in Stage 2. Where you find a difference, consider whether that could be the reason for your current problems. For specific challenges look to Lessons #7–12. Lesson #12, in particular, can help you pinpoint a problem if you are unsure what is causing the struggle.

What is different about this resource?

The Star Team Dynamics approach balances its focus on the people and the process. We suggest how to work with each team member's needs at every step of the way in order to assure commitment, energy, focus and enthusiasm. We respect the intelligence and diversity of team members, and the years of experience of managers, and we seek to help each make the transition. Finally, we provide very practical tools, techniques and processes to set up your structures in a way that will be both resilient and responsive to the warp speed and information avalanche of these amazing times.

The 1990's have taught us many important lessons about teams. If we in the business community heed them . . . if we develop our ability to better plan for teams and better prepare our team members . . . we will not only face less struggle and angst, but also be leaders in the new millennium.

J.R.B.
Chicago
1998

Prologue:

Creating Tomorrow's Teams Today — In Yesterday's Culture

★ Impact on the Workforce
★ Business Tradition vs. Business Future
★ The Star Team℠ Dynamics

Stage I:
The Decision To Launch Into A Team Based Culture

irtual reality. Internet. Information doubling every five years. Everything is changing — fast! But business cultures are having a hard time keeping up.

Business finds itself at an interesting new spot. Its long-standing structure, evolved from the military model, is based on a rigid hierarchical system. Managers hold the information, which they use to help them make decisions, then they *tell* employees what to do. A good employee is one who follows instructions to the letter.

This authoritarian business culture fosters dependency, especially in support staff. A common managerial message is: "Just do what I tell you to do." This approach worked well in the In-dustrial Age, which popularized the notion that people are cogs in the manufacturing wheel. Employees were not to think much, just follow orders. All responsibility for thinking was left to the manager. Therein lay the sys-tem's major flaw. What happened when a model em-ployee — a top performer who followed directions well — was rewarded by being promoted to man-ager? Suddenly this new manager needed to grasp the big picture, to be able to assess situations con-sidering many different inputs, perspectives and facts, and make decisions about where to go in uncharted territory. A substantial challenge for every new manager.

However, today's challenge is much grander. With information so much more available to *everyone in all aspects of life,* we've all become more skilled in how to make decisions. In our personal lives our decisions have changed. With the information explosion has come increased deci-sion complexity. For instance, just a couple of decades ago, we would just put our money into a savings account at the bank. Now there are multiple types of checking accounts, money markets, bounce proof ac-counts, CD's, ATM's, and we can go to our banks to buy stocks and plan our estates and trusts. Dealing with money is no longer a simple matter.

Impact on the Workforce

Today's employees come to work with more complex decision-making skills. They are used to thinking more independently and making choices. They are used to having access to information. They are the best educated workforce ever. And they're not likely to shut down those skills while they're at work.

Today's business cultures are in transition. With one foot in the Industrial Age, the other in the Information Age, and arms reaching out to the Knowledge Age, it's no wonder that workers and businesses are feeling the pull.

Business Tradition vs. Business Future

As society evolves from the Information Age to the Knowledge Age, what you know is no longer as important as what you understand and do with it. This profound shift in the business culture, coupled with the fundamental change in workforce skills and expectations, demands new models for how management and employees work together.

The Authoritarian Approach

Tasks and functions are the focus of the authoritarian approach. In this organizational style, managers tell employees what to do. Decisions are made from the top down.

The Teams Approach

When W. Edwards Deming returned from studying the Japanese business philosophy, he was asked what they had taught him. Without looking up from his dinner, he replied, "People are important."[1]

The focus of teams is people and results. The team has more input into how to do the job. Decisions can be made in multiple ways, from group consensus to leader-led.

The turnaround success of Japanese business due to the use of "quality circles" or teams has impressed American businesses, causing rethinking of the hierarchical Industrial Age organizational model. The focus of the Japanese teams has been *Kaizen*, or continuous improvement, with full contribution from the rank and file. Due to this participation, Japanese business succeeded in turning its reputation for shoddy, cheap product manufacturing to one of undisputed leadership in producing some of the world's highest quality and most sophisticated products.

However, as the 1990's have proven, just *having* teams is not the answer. Perhaps the "secret," if there is one, lies in creating a dynamic culture in each organization. A culture where both the people and the business are constantly evolving into their ideal state. A culture that strikes a balance between some traditional hierarchical and teams structure. A star shaped organization offers an ideal structural model.

The Star Team℠ Dynamics

A star is an entity with a fire in the middle that radiates out to all of its points and sends a glow or light out to others. Unlike the traditional triangle or pyramid shaped organization, the star shaped organization is built on strong interrelationships among its people, its departments and its customers. When you draw a star (see Figure 1), you see that it takes a continuous line to create the whole design. And you end up back at the spot where you began — tying it all together. This star model can be applied to an entire organization or to the teams that make up the organization.

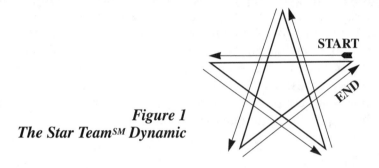

Figure 1
The Star Team℠ Dynamic

The star based structure synthesizes what worked in the hierarchical organization with the interdependency of the new dynamic organization. In the Star Team℠ model (see Figure 2), each triangle of the star

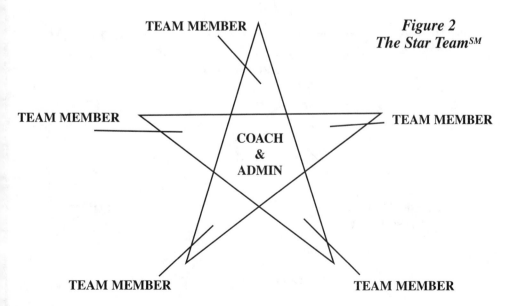

Figure 2
The Star Team℠

TEAM MEMBER

TEAM MEMBER

TEAM MEMBER

COACH
&
ADMIN

TEAM MEMBER

TEAM MEMBER

represents an individual member of the team. Each member has his or her own area of specialty; however, all members are integral to and dependent on one another to complete the whole. The center area of the star is where members come together for meetings, communications and collaboration — where the team creates the synergy, the enthusiasm, the fire. Depending on the group's needs, the center area can also represent administrative support and the team coach. (See Lesson #5 for various new roles for the traditional manager position.)

In the Star Organization model (see Figure 3), the points represent the organization's various departments or functional teams. The center area represents the gathering point for meetings and communication, or where cross-functional teams (made up of representatives from each team) come together to collaborate on specific projects or tasks.

A large organization can be represented by a constellation of stars. Each star has its own unique characteristics, colors and purpose. Like stars in the sky, these can be seen in formations. In the business sky, each corporation's configuration is analogous to a constellation that represents the corporation's unique purpose and vision.

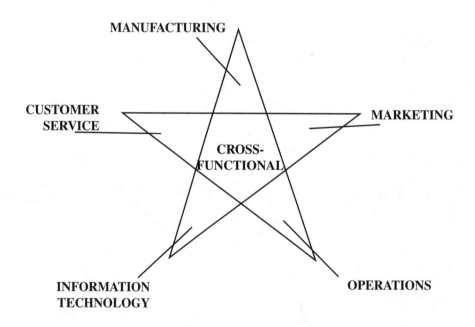

Figure 3
Star Organization

EVOLVING INTO A STAR TEAM℠

In *The Seven Habits of Highly Effective People,*[2] Stephen Covey describes the three stages of human development. As a species, we have the ability to make choices in our development. This unusual characteristic and option is not available to most other species.

The first stage is *Dependence*. Here we need instruction from others in order to function. We do not trust ourselves to decide. We trust only the other person to make decisions and give directions. However, after some experience, we become more capable and confident to function on our own. In this second stage, *Independence*, people have learned from their mistakes and training and feel self-sufficient. However, they may also not be trusting of others, viewing them as competitors.

Apply this thought to today's workers. Can you think of people who have been at the "dependent" stage for their entire work life? They need a lot of instruction and are afraid to make a decision on their own. Can you think of workers who are confident about their jobs while spending time talking negatively and being suspicious about others? Can you see how the hierarchical structure supports both of these developmental levels?

What does the interaction of dependent and independent people create? In business we call it office politics and backstabbing. In the psychological world it is called dysfunction and codependence. The bottom line is that workers are afraid to offer their best ideas, trust others, or go the extra mile. They have painfully learned to either keep quiet or go behind people's backs to get what they want. This is the culture fostered by the hierarchical structure.

It is the right time for many organizations to evolve into the third stage: *Interdependence.* This stage takes the best of the first two stages: the trust one must have to be dependent on others, combined with the self-mastery and self-discipline of independence. To create an environment that fosters growth into interdependence, we must look at our organizations from top to bottom and bottom to top. Find areas where trust, open communications, growth and cooperation are not supported and make conscious choices to reverse the negativity. Then create the Star Teams^{SM} culture to advance everyone to blossom to their full potential. Star Teams^{SM} are not simply "anointed" and performing overnight at high levels. They must be nurtured with thoughtful planning, training, self-discipline and a sense of adventure.

This book will help you look at your organization and guide you through the decision-making and planning process needed to create this environment. You will also learn very practical techniques for helping team members learn to work together interdependently. Because this is a process of maturation, people will not suddenly be terrific Star Team^{SM} players. They will grow into it with support, patience and understanding from one another and from those who guide them.

NOTES

1 Harvey Robbins and Michael Finley, *Why Teams Don't Work.* (Princeton, NJ: Pacesetter Books, 1995), 11.
2 Steven R. Covey, *The Seven Habits of Highly Effective People* (New York: Simon & Schuster, 1989), 49–51.

Lesson #1:

Know When Teams Are The Best Strategy For You

Stage 1:
The Decision To Launch Into A Team Based Culture

The use of teams can be either a fizzling fad or a dynamic energy ball which propels companies to the top in profits, market share and customer satisfaction.

What makes the difference? Based on interviews and years of work with myriad companies of all sizes across the country, we have identified 12 lessons that are critical to creating the interdependence that leads to exceptional performance. The first lesson is to honestly size up your situation in order to determine whether the team structure will work for you.

Reasons for Using Teams

Organizations have had many different reasons for exploring teams as a solution to the challenges they were facing. Check all that apply to your situation:

- ❐ A flattening of your organization.
- ❐ Fewer people must now accomplish more.
- ❐ Unsatisfactory customer satisfaction ratings.
- ❐ Competition is cutting into your business.
- ❐ Coordination is essential — and the "right hand" doesn't know what the "left hand" is doing.
- ❐ Quality depends on cooperating — and your people aren't.
- ❐ Better solutions are needed to problems and challenges.
- ❐ Departments that are interdependent are inconsiderate of one another.
- ❐ Your work process flow — isn't.
- ❐ Employees showing symptoms of rebellion against management (examples: high turnover, sabotage, the gossip network teeming with negativity).
- ❐ Work is too complex and demanding. Managers can't possibly make all the decisions.
- ❐ Employees have expertise and know-how about how things should be done.
- ❐ Employees do not have time to wait for manager's instructions.
- ❐ Employees indicate their morale would improve if they had a say in how things get done.
- ❐ You've tried everything else, and nothing has worked.

Checking even one box above can be an indicator that it is time to consider using teams. If you see these or other indications that teams are a possible strategy for your organization, it's time to turn the page.

Fundamental Questions

Why do you want to create a team? Rather than just plunging in and assigning teams, it's better to begin by thoughtfully considering these important basic, sometimes tough, questions.

> What do you want to accomplish that you have not yet been able to?
> What do you want more of? Less of?
> What do you want done differently?
> What do you expect your team(s) to accomplish?
> What kind of a team is necessary to accomplish that goal?
> What changes in the organization need to be made to support teams?
> How can you organize and nurture teams?

Knowing what you want to accomplish — and designing a plan to get there — are vital to setting teams up for exceptional performance. Sound basic? Maybe so. But many organizations in the 1990's skipped this step. All too often, teams came about because an executive read about them in a book, or heard about the success of others, and decided to implement teams right away in his or her own organization. Well intentioned, but often a recipe for failure. There is much to know and consider before starting teams.

What Is a "Team"?

Teams are not new. People have been working together since the second person was created. Here is our definition of a team.

A Team:
Two or more people who when working together can synergistically realize the goal better than if they worked separately.

A key word here is "synergistically." Many people who work side by side do not work together synergistically — in other words, so that their combined efforts are greater than the total of what they accomplish individually. In the 1990's, many who called themselves teams were really only groups of people who came together to work or report on their work. In the Information Age, they shared information, and that did bring them one step closer to being teams. But in the Knowledge Age, developing teams has new challenges. There is both good and bad news.

The Bad News First: What We Are Up Against

In our research and that of others, the most common reason for early failure or struggle in team development was that the "team" structure was imposed on a group — they were simply anointed as teams and told they were now expected to function as a team. For most North Americans, raised in a culture of rugged individualism, being placed on a team in a work situation is 180 degrees removed from their comfort zone.

The lessons from the Industrial Age are ingrained. Industrial Age people are not trained in collaboration. They are predisposed to thinking in terms of "me" rather than "we," and more focused on individual rather than collective success.

FROM WHENCE WE CAME . . .

As a result of this individualistic culture, overlaid on the hierarchical structure, employees have been rewarded for using these time-tested beliefs and practices.

Old Top 10 Survival Tactics
1. I just work here. They don't pay me to think.
2. That's not my job.
3. We've always done it this way.
4. It's not my fault.
5. Don't listen to others — our ideas are better than theirs anyway.
6. Don't trust others — they may be out to get you.
7 Information is power — guard it carefully.
8. Cut others down to build your own image.
9. Whoever shouts the loudest or talks the longest — wins.
10. The goal is to get to the top — no matter who you have to trample to get there.

Business Success is a Singular Sport

Or so we were taught. After all, teamwork runs counter to the hierarchical, authoritarian business culture in which we were all raised. Most of us learned early on that in order to survive, let alone thrive, we must excel as individuals.

Success as a team member requires a major shift. We may need to tap into parts of us that have not been used much in the past, namely, focusing on altruism, setting the ego aside, seeking cooperation, collaborating, really listening for understanding, and sharing praise. This shift in attitudes and behaviors may feel uncomfortable at first. It may be hard to remember to put them into practice, because we are so used to listening to "self-centered radio" — WII-FM (What's In It For Me).

But efforts to make it work are rewarded. As a team, we also get to share the hard times. Others can help come up with solutions. In pressure situations, everyone can pitch in to help. And what a deeper sense of satisfaction we gain when we have worked together to accomplish the goal. The celebrations are much more fun, too.

GETTING PEOPLE TO CHANGE

In 1963 the Surgeon General put a warning on cigarettes to inform the public that cigarettes kill. When did group behavior change? One of the first indicators that group behavior would change due to this warning was in 1993 — a full 30 years later — when smoking was banned on many airline flights.

The moral? It takes a long time for groups to change — even in a life-threatening situation.

People change when they hurt enough and they have to change.
When people learn enough, they want to change.
When they receive enough information, they are able to change.
—Source Unknown

The special challenge now for anyone intent on establishing a team culture is that no matter what strategy you use to change, you are suffering from time compression. You do not have the luxury of a generation in which to blend the changes. Businesses must respond and often totally change their cultures in just a few years. What does this mean to each individual? Everyone must learn how to think and behave in new ways. How jobs are done will be changing. How individuals relate to each other will be different. The role of managers will greatly change. The rules will change. This is not an easy transformation to ask people to make.

THE "ME" VS. "WE" BALANCE

In evolving into a "we" focused environment, there is still a need to keep some of the "me" focus. The author initially thought it would be necessary to give up the self focus, but now realizes the importance of maintaining a balance of each. The key is to know how much of each to have at what time.

In a new team, participants start with a heavier "me" focus until they get to know and trust the other team members. The "we" comes into play most during the "Norming" and "Performing" stages (see Lesson #2). However, there must be an intent toward seeking the "we" even at the first two stages, or the team will never coalesce. Team members will be relieved to know that they do not have to totally change everything about themselves all at once!

The Good News: The Payoff

Given that hard work — and even struggle — may be needed to create this new culture, what is the payoff? Successful application of a team-based culture has shown results of many different types:

- XEROX experienced a 30% productivity gain.
- Federal Express cut mistakes by 13%.
- Milwaukee Mutual Insurance lowered operating costs and sped up processing time considerably.
- Westinghouse reduced cycle time from 12 down to 2 weeks.
- K Shoes increased output per employee by 19%.
- Harris Electronics achieved an 18% reduction in costs.
- Texas Instruments in Malaysia reduced defects from 100 parts per million to 20 parts per million.
- UCAR Carbon reduced inventory by 50% and is on its way to saving $10 million annually through teamwork productivity improvements.[1]

Cases In Point

DENNEN STEEL: Teams resulted in an increase in productivity, greater tonnage per man-hour shipped, an increase in pieces shipped, and reduced down time. Productivity and efficiency have gone up so much that one night shift team was able to be eliminated. Through natural attrition and reshuffling of staffers, everyone ended up in more desirable situations.

WELCH ALLYN: Decisions made by this medical equipment company's Imaging Products team over a three year period resulted in the team reducing its size by half, while still producing at the same level. Each time a team member would leave or get promoted, the team made a decision about how to handle the tasks formerly handled by that person. Through teamwork, the members developed a strong sense of company and team goals. From this perspective, the team chose to seek the smaller, more efficient productivity profile.

MASSACHUSETTS INSTITUTE OF TECHNOLOGY: As the authors of *The Superteam Solution* noted, "Europe, which proportionately has a large number of very brilliant but individualistic scientists, has won relatively few Nobel Prizes, whereas MIT, the first research center to use teams seriously to conduct scientific research, has had seventeen. We can't prove it, but there seems to be a lesson there. 'Close cooperation is better than genius' say the Americans."[2]

Successful results from the use of teams are as varied as the goals are. The promise for success and bottom line results is real — if the right decisions are made.

PEOPLE BENEFITS

What's in it for employees?

+ More input into the outcome
+ Greater feeling of ownership and pride
+ Feel more a part of the solution
+ Greater sense of control about job, process and end result
+ Opportunity to share the hard times
+ Assistance in coming up with solutions
+ Support in "pressure cooker" times as everyone pitches in to help
+ Deeper sense of satisfaction from having worked together to accomplish the goal
+ Feel the reward of accomplishing goals once considered unattainable
+ Celebrations are much more fun

What's in it for managers?

+ Employees often solve their own problems without needing manager's help
+ No longer need to have all the answers
+ Don't have to have all the accountability
+ Opportunity to step back from the detail and view the "big picture"
+ More time available for planning
+ More time to get **own** job done

+ More reward from mentoring/coaching, i.e. watching people grow
+ Excitement of growth
+ May get to play any of five new roles (see Lesson #5)

When NOT to Use Teams

Teams are not the solution for all that ails business. Here are some situations when the individualistic approach is best:

1. SPECIFIC EFFICIENCY

If one person can get a job done better or more efficiently by themselves, then don't consider a team. Two important factors are: if that person is the only one with the information or expertise, or if there is no concern about others' buy-in with the outcome. In banking, there are many jobs that function better independently, such as tellers or those who check numbers. Data entry positions may lend themselves more to independence. But even in these cases, any of these people may need to be on a team, if they are to design a new process or solve a problem that affects the entire department.

2. CERTAIN DECISIONS

There are times when decisions are best made by one person and not in a collaborative environment. One case is in emergencies or situations when time demands prohibit collaboration. A single person should decide whenever the decision:

- Must be made very quickly.
- Is not very important.
- Is vital to only a few people.
- Does not need others' buy-in in order to implement it well.

3. EXTREME TIME CRUNCHES

When time demands prevent collaboration, then one person must act. However, this can become a trap. Most workers today feel they have too much to do in the time available. So someone could always say, "Sorry, there just was not enough time to call a team meeting."

4. SINGULAR STAKEHOLDERS

A decision where the main stakeholder has the most to risk should be made by one person. As an example, if the owner of a privately held company is considering whether to sell the company, it may be most appropriate for that person to decide. But even in this case, the individual would be well advised to form a team to help examine the decision.

> Not everything needs to be a team decision. If it did, business would come to a sudden halt.

When Teams Are Right For You

In summary, the first lesson is deciding if teams are right for your situation. Teams are the best strategic tool when:

- ❐ Buy-in is important for implementation
- ❐ More and better ideas are needed
- ❐ Fewer people must accomplish the same or bigger goals
- ❐ Streamlining needs to happen
- ❐ Productivity needs to rise
- ❐ Continuous improvement is an important competitive edge
- ❐ People's work is interdependent
- ❐ Cooperation among individuals or groups is critical
- ❐ A problem arises that affects multiple people or departments
- ❐ People close to the situation or problem could get involved to improve or fix it
- ❐ Employees are asking to have input

NOTES

1. Richard S. Wellins, William C. Byham, and George R. Dixon, *Inside Teams* (San Francisco: Jossey-Bass, Inc., 1994).
2. Colin Hastings, Peter Bixby, Rani Chaudhry-Lawton, *The Superteam Solution* (San Diego: University Associates, Inc., 1987), 106.

Lesson #2

Plan for the Critical Transition into Star Teams^{SM}

Part I: The Process — Creating a Team-Based Culture

★ An Option: Activity Analysis

★ A Suggested Option: The Pioneer Approach

★ Not Optional: Establish a Worthy Goal

★ Continuous Team Training is Critical

★ Using the 4 Stages of Team Development to Help the Process

Part II: The People — Transforming Individualists Into Star Team^{SM} Players

★ Understanding & Overcoming Resistance

★ Change Styles: Different Strokes for Different Folks

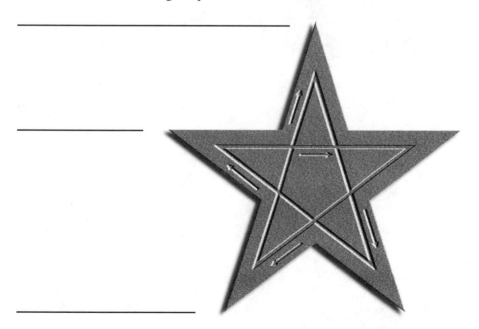

Stage II:
Planning And Designing A Star Team^{SM} Culture

*A*fter deciding that the organization needed to be in teams, many 1990's managers "took charge" of the change. This is typical of Industrial Age thinking.

Whenever a manager saw a need for a change, he decided what it should be, then told the employee to make the change and assumed it was done and done well. In today's world, because workers customarily make more decisions, have more knowledge and feel more empowered in themselves, they feel a need to be part of decision-making in order to have buy-in. A painful lesson learned is that, to successfully make the change into teams, employees need to be involved in designing the process. And, they need time to accept and adjust to new roles and relationships.

Part I: The Process — Creating a Team-Based Culture

A legacy of our Industrial Age mentality is that we think people are like machines and processes. If we put them together, i.e. assemble them, that should be enough to make the process function. We keep looking for the "On" button, in the hope that we can then just walk away and they (like a machine) will produce our expected outcome.

People need education, coaching, guidance and nurturing to successfully make the transition to teams. A collaborative, empowered teams environment is 180 degrees away from the hierarchical, "boss-driven" culture. Changing to a team-based culture means changing generations of business habits, expectations and role definitions.

Intellectually knowing and realizing that we need to change to teams as a tool to thrive in the future is one thing. But we need to help ourselves and our colleagues quickly make the transition. We do not have a generation or even a decade to do so. We have only a few years to transform our people into highly productive, collaborative teams.

Nevertheless, in case after case, the struggle and failure of teams happens when the company rushes into the process. So planning for an efficient transformation is critical.

Case

Steve Johns, owner of PMI PRINTMAILERS, is a typical example. He shares his story so others don't have to struggle like he and his staff did.

Over a one-year period, Steve read books about, talked to others and went to workshops on how to use teams. He liked the idea, but was not convinced that teams would work in his industry, until he visited an industry colleague's operation. This shop was very successful with the team approach. Steve asked staffers how long they thought it would take to implement teams. They answered with a question: "How long will it take to move your equipment around?" "Over the weekend," he replied.

Shortly after he returned home, he announced the change to a team structure, worked with his staff to reorganize the equipment in the way they thought best, and put them through some training. Then he stood back to watch for the expected increase in productivity, decrease in mistakes, and newly enthusiastic and accountable employees. Hardly the actual results. Instead, he lost 40% of his staff in the first year, morale fell to an all-time low and there were no fantastic bottom line results.

A smart businessman who founded two other successful companies, Steve learned a very important lesson and would like to pass it on.

What He Learned

Start slow and be very patient in order to effect the best kind of change. Plan it out and get the staff's buy-in at every step.

Since slowing down, conducting more training, and hiring people with a team focus, Steve says that after three years he is finally seeing the kind of results he was initially looking for.

THE RESULTS

- Employees have a deep sense of "ownership" and focus on helping the company succeed.
- They understand how their team makes money.
- They have learned how to get and manage larger accounts.
- They have learned how to be efficient, low cost producers.

Even though his industry has become highly competitive, Steve sees that 25% growth for his company this year is a reasonable expectation given the sophistication his teams now have.

An Option: Activity Analysis

Some find it a useful tool to conduct an Activity Analysis process first. This tool makes it possible to go into the team building process from a needs based approach. In this process, each department analyzes its activities/tasks, then decides:

- The purpose or goal of each task.
- Whether each task is necessary.
- What can be streamlined or omitted.

Case

ALEXIAN BROTHERS MEDICAL CENTER, a health care facility of 2000 employees, had a goal of increasing service and keeping balanced financials — a tough challenge within the managed care environment. A year was spent in completing the Activity Analysis Process, which was done by forming cross functional teams to look at the tasks.

What They Learned
- Keep the focus on the positive outcomes.
- Keep everyone informed of the status and results of each team's work.
- Keep no secrets.
- Have thorough training in:
    How to analyze activities
    How to work together on a team, especially the communications and relationship part
    How to run meetings

Marne Bonomo, Director of Patient Registration and a leader in developing teams at Alexian Brothers, recommends the book *Activity-Based Management For Service Industries, Government Entities, and Nonprofit Organizations.*[1]

Even though cutting jobs was not one of the motives of the analysis at Alexian Brothers, the nurses still expressed skepticism and resistance. The situation was addressed by having informative meetings reporting on the results of each team. In addition, each team came up with its own suggestions for improvements or changes.

This approach worked well for Alexian Brothers because it provided a way to improve service and systems, while developing teams with an important purpose. The use of teams has now been expanded as a part of the solution to the analysis. The staff sees the use of teams as an evolving, flexible and expanding tool to help them meet their goals.

Be aware that the Activity Analysis can take considerable time. For Alexian Brothers, the process took about one year.

The challenge in using the Activity Analysis process is that staff may feel the ultimate motive is to eliminate positions or people.

SUGGESTION
If you use Activity Analysis where staff teams analyze their activities, **do not have the ulterior motive of cutting jobs.**

A Suggested Option: The Pioneer Approach

Knowing the pitfalls of attempting to create a team based environment overnight, others have successfully used the Pioneer Approach to help ease the way. By carefully choosing a department or group with pioneer characteristics as the first pilot group, you can assure a better adaptation by the whole organization.

Pioneer Characteristics:
- Open to new ideas and approaches
- Have good rapport within the group
- Share a worthy goal to achieve as a team
- Have worked together for awhile (not essential, but very helpful)

Case

DENNEN STEEL wanted to improve its delivery systems and manufacturing process. The executive team felt they could accomplish this best by using the intelligence of the employees who work face to face with the systems and equipment. Rather than just "empowering" the staff, they wanted to form them into empowered teams. They chose a department which had worked together for four years, had showed leadership in the past, and was made up of sincere and caring employees.

Even with these characteristics, the group's first few meetings were filled with anger and fighting. This was when they realized they didn't know the difference between a group and team, and how to work together as a true team. They then immersed themselves in team building training. In practicing what they learned from the training, they were able to agree on goals, an implementation process, and ways to work together. They began to see real progress and feel a new sense of involvement and pride in their work.

This eight month pioneering adventure set a course for the teams that followed them, preventing others from having to experience the same pain and loss of time. As the second team prepared for its adventure, members were eager with anticipation based on the resulting success of their colleagues. The second time around, training was made mandatory.

Not Optional: Establish a Worthy Goal

A team without a purpose
is a **party!**
paid for by the company.

Having a specific, worthy goal for each team is vital. Answer the following questions (see your earlier thoughts under Fundamental Questions in Lesson #1 for some ideas):

- What do you want to accomplish that you have not yet been able to?
- What do you want more of? Less of?
- What different results do you want?
- What is a worthy goal worth achieving?

Make sure the team has a purpose and goal that is worthwhile. Look for projects that can really have an impact on company performance. Examples: correcting customer dissatisfaction, reducing waste, saving time or money, speeding up processes. (See suggestions below for writing the goals).

Case

A large high-tech company headquartered in the Chicago area wanted to establish teams. They decided to give the new teams practice before working on any important issues. (Management feared the teams might make poor decisions due to inexperience.) So the teams were given small tasks. However, team participants had low interest in committing time to such trivial goals. This low commitment affected team member meeting attendance and follow-through on action items. Friction developed in teams where some members were committed to the exercise and others were not. This set a negative precedent for the team experience when real issues needed to be addressed.

CHOOSE YOUR WORDS AND FOCUS CAREFULLY

Be very careful in choosing the words to describe your goal.

☆ Be Specific

One company set the goal of "improving the quality of our product." They didn't know when they reached the goal. Construct the goal description so you will know when you have reached it. Setting a timeline for completion creates a focus and motivation.

A goal can have a list of sub-goals. Example: *Our goal is to achieve the following quality levels by December 31:*

- 1% or less accidents in the plant
- 2% or less returned product
- At least 2 days reduced in product output cycle time
- A 24 hour or less response time on customer breakdowns

☆ Be Realistic

If the goal is too grandiose, people will not buy into it. For example, when the author was in sales for Control Data, she was one of the top performers nationally one year. The next year, management doubled her quota, then reorganized her territory taking major segments away. The goal was unrealistic. She lost momentum and morale, and left the company halfway through the year.

☆ *Make It Measurable or Monitorable*

It is always easier to see progress when looking at a measurable goal. However, many goals are hard to measure. Look for ways to monitor progress with specific milestones even for these more ambiguous goals.

Staying Focused on the Goal

When focus drifts from the goal, problems arise. "The team had raised — or had allowed to become raised — some other issue or focus above the team's performance objective."[2]

Issues such as:

- Who is in charge, power or control
- An individual pushing their agenda issue
- A political issue

are typical of the hierarchical structure and the dependent/independent maturation stages. When the team has a worthy goal to focus on, it is easier to leave egos behind and progress to the Star Team[SM] level.

Continuous Team Training is Critical

Many teams in the 1990's had the foresight to begin the team building process with training. However, most stopped after the initial training program. Management's thought process usually reasoned, "Once we have them trained, all we have to do is just let them go do it." That perspective ignores the fact that a major change in human behavior and perspective is being asked for. People need continual reinforcement, reminders and support to make the transition. That is why the training *after* the initial training can be the most critical to assure true behavior, role and perspective change.

WHAT TO INCLUDE

The initial curriculum depends on any previous training the employees have received.

Following is a suggested minimal foundation for first time teams.

Initial Team Training

- The benefits of using teams
- Why should we use teams now?
- How to define our goal and set milestones and measurements
- Types of Knowledge Age teams

- Putting together a new team — getting to know each other differently
- The typical developmental stages of a team
- What roles help the team members handle their own process more effectively?
- Helping everyone through this change
- Setting up our Communication Agreements
- How to use Sponsors or Ambassadors to assure influential support (see Lesson #5: The New Role of Management)

Later in the Process

- How to increase problem solving creativity and constructiveness
- Conflict vs. a difference of opinion
- Doing things differently: expanding your team's risk-taking ability
- Working together to better serve the customer
- Motivating everyone to participate
- Leading vs. following vs. participating
- Team leadership: a new skill
- Evolving into Self-Directed Teams
- Team assessment for continual improvement in cooperation

Relationships

- Understanding Synergy Builders and learning to avoid Synergy Busters
- The In vs. the Out group
- How to build trust in a team
- Building team spirit
- How to handle emotionally charged team meetings
- Increasing team ability to work together
- Creating interteam cooperation
- Competition vs. cooperation
- How to deal with or remove a disruptive team member

Communications

- Getting all personalities on the team to communicate better (and work together better)
- Beyond words: how to listen for the real meaning
- Creating clear communications
- Handling emotional communications
- Informal communications, spontaneous meetings and other tools to increase team communications

Management Training

In addition, managers want and need to know about:

- Why and when to use teams as a business strategy
- Creating employee buy-in
- Helping your team through change
- How to get commitment to creating a team based culture
- Empowerment questions: How to decide who should have power and make decisions
- Manager, Team Leader, Member: What is my role?
- Most appropriate leadership styles for each type of team
- Finding out what motivates people
- Coaching: How to teach people to think in new ways

WHO SHOULD DELIVER THE TRAINING?

Case

WELCH ALLYN recognized the importance of training, so some staffers were sent to get certified as trainers in a nationally known training firm's program. Welch's staff were not professional trainers. After being certified, they did their best to relay the messages and concepts of the training. The challenging part came when facilitation skills were needed to help with the real-life interpersonal situations. They struggled with handling the conflicts and other disruptive behaviors. Of the four pilot teams started at Welch Allyn, only one survived. Michael Dahlin attributes that team's success to its strong commitment to "tough it out."

Applying the concepts and techniques in real life is much harder than practicing in training program role plays. The "getting along" aspect of teams is usually the biggest challenge. In most cases the tough relationship issues come out during the implementation stage. That is where expert and objective facilitation skills are needed to deal with challenges such as anger, resistance, defensiveness, personal verbal attacks, or power struggles.

For best results, utilize trained facilitators or team coaches who work with each team on a regular basis until the teams have really absorbed and are displaying the new team behaviors. Realistically, this may take one to two years. *Remember: team building is a process.* You are asking people to change behavior, values and perspectives they have had their whole lives.

Using the 4 Stages of Team Development to Help the Process

Teams tend to pass through four stages of development, as noted by B.W. Tuckerman.[3] He describes them as "forming, storming, norming and performing." Learning to recognize these stages can help alleviate fears, such as "We're falling apart!" rather than, "Ah yes, we are passing through the storming phase. What do we need to know to help us through this stage?"

There are different questions and issues at each stage. Find ways at each stage to answer these questions:

Forming	Why are we each here? What is this team all about? What is the goal?
Storming	What does the team want from me? (What am I supposed to do? What is my role?) What do I want from the team?
Norming	How will we all get along? What is our method of operation? What approach/process are we going to use?
Performing	Am I a valued part of this team? Are my efforts helping the team reach the goals? What measures do we use to determine our success?

USE TRAINING AT EACH STAGE

Training can be delivered to help teams at each stage. This will allow growth to happen through learning, and prevent painful mistakes. Examples:

Forming Stage
- The benefits of using teams
- Why we should use teams now
- How to define our goal and set milestones and measurements
- Types of Knowledge Age teams

- Putting together a new team — getting to know each other differently
- The typical developmental stages of a team
- Helping ourselves through this change
- Setting up our Communication Agreements

Storming Stage

- What roles help team members handle their own process more effectively
- How to increase problem solving creativity and constructiveness
- Conflict vs. a difference of opinion
- Handling emotional communications
- Getting all personalities on the team to communicate better (and work together better)
- Doing things differently: expanding your team's risk-taking ability
- Working together to better serve the customer
- Motivating everyone to participate
- Leading vs. following vs. participating
- Team leadership: a new skill
- How to build trust in a team
- How to handle emotionally charged team meetings
- Competition vs. cooperation

Norming Stage

- How to use Sponsors or Ambassadors to assure influential support (see Lesson #5: The New Role of Management)
- Evolving into Self-Directed Teams
- Team assessment for continual improvement in cooperation
- Understanding Synergy Builders and learning to avoid Synergy Busters
- The In vs. the Out group
- Building team spirit
- Increasing team ability to work together
- Creating interteam cooperation
- How to deal with or remove a disruptive team member
- Beyond words: how to listen for the real meaning
- Creating clear communications

Performing Stage

- Informal communications, spontaneous meetings and other tools to increase team communications
- Brainstorm on how we want to acknowledge and reward ourselves

Part II: The People —
Transforming Individualists Into Star Team^{SM} Players

Resistance may arise as you face the challenge of helping yourself and others move from focusing on the "me" to the "we."

Author's Case

Have you ever had one of those great ideas that you're convinced everyone else will love too? One of my great ideas came while I served as an officer of the Professional Speakers of Illinois. I thought, "Let's get together with the top officers of other Chicago meetings industry organizations on a regular basis to discuss industry issues and coordinate our programs." I felt this brain trust would provide a forum to address industry issues, learn from each other and prevent dueling events on the same day competing for the same participants. I saw this as the formation of a meetings industry team. This very same concept had worked in Denver, so I was sure it would work in Chicago.

At the first meeting I was excitedly telling everyone about all the benefits of forming the group. Then I immediately jumped into planning for the first joint event. In my zealousness, I failed to notice that one of the participants, the head of one of the largest industry organizations, was shifting uneasily in his seat and looking agitated. Suddenly he blurted out, "It looks to me that this organization will benefit all of you, but be a drain on us." During a deafening silence, my mind raced searching for something to say in response. I realized he was right. The benefits were indeed lopsided. I had not looked at it from his point of view. In trying to save the moment, I listed a variety of indirect ways his organization could benefit, but it was clear he was not buying it.

Not long afterward, I was only half surprised to receive a letter from him saying his association would not be signing on as a part of the team. In the midst of my disappointment, I asked myself, "What did I learn?" My lesson was that in order to create a true team, everyone must see what the payoff is for them, or they will not contribute. Even in teams, people must know WIIFM (What's In It For Me). In other words, in teams, the "we" begins with "me."

Understanding & Overcoming Resistance

Fear of the unknown causes people to act in a defensive way. Following are six most common resistance behaviors and how to overcome them.

RESISTANCE #1

People focus first on what they have to give up.

To Overcome It

Be aware that this is a normal reaction. Emphasize what people are NOT giving up. Have them think about what they can gain by moving into a team environment. Often the core of this concern is a focus on or obsession about "the change." Begin the discussion with what is staying the same. Make long lists or have them make lists of what is not changing.

RESISTANCE #2

People are concerned that they don't have enough resources.

To Overcome It

Find out what they think they need — make lists. Ask what they will be able to do (very specifically) as a result of having that resource. If they are able to describe a result, have everyone weigh the cost with the benefit and make a decision or prioritize which resources to acquire. This recognizes people's needs and allows everyone to deal with them in a logical way.

RESISTANCE #3

People tend to feel awkward, ill at ease and uncomfortable while going through change.

To Overcome It

Laugh at ourselves! Lighten up! Recognize the fact that we all may feel uncomfortable during this new adventure. Then allow everyone to step outside of the situation mentally, and observe themselves. Hopefully some humor can be seen in the situation and in themselves.

Be creative! The staff at one hospital, very upset because their facility had been bought by a large medical conglomerate, did not know whether their jobs would be secure. They also knew they would not know for awhile. So what did they do to creatively communicate their discomfort and yet laugh at themselves? They put a large goblet of M&M's at the nurses station. The agreement was that whenever people were really bothered by the situation, they would pick out the appropriate amount of M&M's to show their level of frustration. Others in the area could see their action and could laugh with them, saying "Ah, it's a 10 M&M day!" and offer some support.

Be an Adventurer! View this new way of relating to one another as an adventure. See yourself as an explorer or pioneer — never quite knowing what is around the next corner, but looking with anticipation and eagerness.

RESISTANCE #4

People can handle only so much change.

There comes a point where people will figuratively "hit the wall." They can't take another change. That moment may come when the person is asked to attend yet another team meeting. Like the proverbial straw that broke the camel's back, the person may fly off the handle over a seemingly small request.

To Overcome It

Be prepared to approach the high emotion with Care, Concern and Calmness. Let them know you care about their distress with the situation at hand. Then share your concern that this may also be related to all the changes that are underway. You want them to be able to successfully cope with the immediate challenge as well as any others that may arise. Ask what you or others can do to help.

As you calmly express your care and concern, they will probably calm down. Often people just need to vent — to talk to someone who understands and will listen. Many times they don't need for anything to be done differently. Just talking may relieve their pent-up emotions.

RESISTANCE #5

People may be at different levels of readiness for change.

Due to many factors such as age, amount of change happening at home or a person's change style, people vary in their degree of readiness for a change. For instance, if the in-laws have just moved in, or a new baby arrived and they've just moved into a new house, this person may not be able to handle any change at work. People's reaction to the introduction of teams in times of stress may not reflect how they handled a previous change, when things were stable at home.

To Overcome It

Know your teammates. Know the whole person, not just the part of them that's the function (such as Accountant) they serve in the organization. How can you do this?

Use Meeting Openers

This technique is shared by Enlightened Leadership International, Inc. in its training program "Making Managers into Leaders." It involves beginning your meetings with a quick question. In this application, we recommend it be fun and not work related. Some examples:

"What's going on in your life that is exciting that you'd like to share with us?"

"What do you like to do when you're not at work?"

"Where is your favorite vacation spot and what do you like to do there?"

For more examples and tips for successful implementation, turn to Lesson #9.

Support Your Teammates

Spend a little extra time with those who are struggling with their new role, with the goal of:

- Listening to them.
- Empathizing with their point of view.
- Offering information on sources for assistance, if appropriate.
- Focusing on the positive gains from the team focus.
- Helping them take an action step toward the team focus.

Once this action step is taken, people generally feel better and start to focus on the implementation stage.

RESISTANCE #6

If the pressure for change is removed, people revert back to their old behaviors.

Due to any of the resistance reasons cited above, people will still feel more comfortable with the old way of doing things. So when the change agent leaves the office, the person may go back to doing it the old way. Sometimes it is out of habit and people honestly forget.

To Overcome It

Create friendly visible reminders to do things in the new way, such as posters, cartoons, specialty items like mugs with slogans or reminders.

Have everyone go through training on how to work on a team. Then they can support each other with reminders. Help them understand how to give constructive reminders to each other, to keep motivation up for the next time.

What about those who still resist the change?

There will still be those stubborn individuals who don't want to change. Usually their resistance centers around the discomfort of new ways, a lack of self confidence that they can make the change, and a lack of involvement. Try these techniques.

Have a reality check. Tell the truth about the reality of your situation. This goes back to the reasons for moving into teams. For instance, "With our current challenges we cannot continue as we have. So we and you are going to have to change to survive and thrive in our future."

Recall past successes. Say something like: "You have changed in the past and you can do it again. Each phase in your life has caused changes. Some you liked and others may have been unpleasant, but you got through it and hopefully grew through it — learning important lessons that helped you with your future."

Foster participation. Being on the team to analyze what is needed and design the plan and its implementation helps many people adapt to the change. However, some will still say, "Just tell me what you want me to do and I'll do it. I don't want to be on any silly committee or team to hash things out." An effective way to help these people make the change is to keep them well informed of the planning team's progress. Usually these people need to know *why* decisions are made. As they see others excelling on the team, they will not want to be left behind. As soon as they show an openness to learn how to be on a team, get them into training.

Give them time. Do not put these high resisters on the Pioneer Team. Let them watch the first team until it has proven successful. This time of "checking it out" and learning from their colleagues' experience can help them prepare themselves and feel more confident about the change.

THE CHALLENGE IS REAL AND MANAGEABLE

It is realistic to expect that implementing teams may be a challenge. It may be a new and different way of relating. But if people can draw from their previous experience of being on successful teams, they will realize how much they already know that can be adapted to teams in today's environment.

Change Styles: Different Strokes for Different Folks

Thinking that all they had to do was put the process in place — and then individuals would easily change into teams — was a fatal mistake companies made in the 1990's. Unfortunately, most people don't jump at the chance to let go of their current way of doing and being. So how can you help people make the transition? By recognizing their individual needs as they go through their own change process.

Some would say there is a standard cycle that people go through when faced with change. We disagree. In our experience, people handle and approach change in different ways. Following is a look at the four typical change styles — Realist, Collaborator, Goal Seeker and Visionary — including their favorable and unfavorable characteristics, and tips for coping with changing into a team environment. As you read about the four change styles, think about:

Which style is most like you?

Who do you know who is like this style?

What style do you think your own teammates function from?

The Realist

The Plusses + +

To a Realist, information is the key, especially when change is introduced. Realists are great seekers and gatherers of information. They are very practical, focused and thorough. When given a task, a Realist will see it through all of the steps to the end.

The Minuses – –

The Realist's first verbal response is often negative. Typical Realist comments: "This won't work." "The way we have been organized has been working just fine. Why do we need to change?" or the old standard, "But . . . " And they will find a thousand and one reasons not to want to change to a team environment. They will be the skeptics.

Realists may be perceived as too detailed. As an example, a Realist is an important member of an Exploration Team looking into setting up a team culture. But they often annoy others by asking endless questions. When assigned to do research or gather information in order to bring the culture change to fruition, they may tend to "research it to death" by wanting to read more and more data and talk to more organizations who have already been through the change. While other team members are focused on the goal and the deadline, Realists will drive them nuts with their need for more details!

As one of our non-Realist clients wisely pointed out, "The only thing that does not change is the deadline." You still have to accomplish as much, even though all these changes are happening and the deadline is looming. The effect on the Realists is they may feel overwhelmed with trying to do such in-depth research (to make themselves feel better) and still get the rest of their work done. When Realists are threatened or made to feel insecure, such as when the change is actually introduced, their defensive reaction is often to withhold information. Because information to them is power and security, giving them a sense of control, they will be reluctant to share it with others. This can slow down the progress of the team. They'll miss their deadlines, even though in a normal situation they love to meet deadlines. They may keep key information from team members they feel threatened by.

When Realists are extremely fearful or overwhelmed, they react defensively by freezing up. They'll stay in their office, module or work area much more of the time. In meetings, they won't speak out anymore. When you ask for their opinion, they'll just barely respond. They will withdraw.

Overall, Realists struggle the most with change and may take the longest to accept it and be a part of it.

WHAT TO DO IF YOU ARE A REALIST

To help yourself understand and cope with the change:

Volunteer to be on the team to research setting up teams (or whatever the subject might be).

Seek information in writing. To a realist, the spoken word has far less credibility than what is written on paper. The spoken word is easily changed. But once it's on paper, it is committed to. It feels more tangible and concrete. This makes a Realist feel more secure.

Ask questions. Because information is so important to you, ask questions until you feel more comfortable. Please, when you ask the questions, ask them gently. Avoid sarcasm or blaming tones. If you have questions but do not ask them, that can start you into the withdrawal stage. It is much better to stay as an active member of the team in order to make sure your contribution is heard.

Watch others first. You probably will not feel comfortable being the first

Team Leader or Facilitator. A more comfortable role may be Time-keeper or Scribe.

Participate! You have a lot to offer. Get in there and be a part of the team. You will feel better over time.

TECHNIQUES TO HELP YOUR REALIST TEAMMATES

How can you use the Realist's traits in a positive way, and turn their skepticism around?

Invite them to research when that function is necessary.

Explain why the department or organization is moving into teams.

Define step by step how this transition is going to be made. Present the information in an orderly, sequential manner. You can also involve them in the design of the steps, if it is not a team function.

Write down the information. You can say it verbally, but have the documentation or a description of the steps written down.

Relate the old way to the new way. Review what things from the old way will be kept, before discussing what the changes will be. This will allow them to bridge from their comfort zone of the old into the new. Knowing there are no plans to get rid of everything will open them more to consider the changes.

Expect questions and skepticism. Asking questions is how Realists adapt to change. Don't take it personally. Have patience and answer all their questions or help them find the answers.

The Collaborator

The Plusses + +

The Collaborator is a "people" person. When change is introduced, Collaborators are very good at involving other people in it. If change is introduced at a meeting, they will probably be the ones who will watch what's going on with others. They will help draw them out, saying for example, "Well, Fran, what do you think about that? You've been sitting there kind of quietly." People will confide in and trust Collaborators. They are good at bringing the group together, and getting everybody's ideas. They also tend to know who is good at what, so they are good at helping to decide who can play what roles. Like the Realists, they are also thorough. However, the reason they are motivated toward thoroughness is that they want to meet others' expectations.

They are also very good at developing steps. Their steps, however, tend to involve people, not process or documentation. Where the Realist would be designing the analysis process, the Collaborator will be able to say who should do what during all phases of development. The Realist wants to know the "what's" and the "why's," the Collaborators focus on the "who's."

The Minuses – –

Be aware that a Collaborator when threatened tends to get embroiled in the people part of the change. They gather their information from talking to others: "What do you think is going to happen?" "Oh, have you heard?" "Well, I heard Joe said that . . . " They are usually an active part of the gossip mill, spreading information via people. Whether it's true or not. Sharing information with others is how they increase their feelings of security. Because of their security need, they will probably spend more of their day talking to folks, and less of their time doing their job. The less secure they feel, the more they'll need to talk.

Another one of their strengths can turn into a problem when not handled appropriately. When given the challenge of developing the people aspects of a change, they may start to create a bureaucracy. This comes from their need to make sure everyone is well informed and "has a say." The more insecure they are about the change, the more meetings, reports, memos and printouts they will want. Sometimes this goes beyond what makes good sense.

Collaborators will also fight any change in midstream. If you have introduced teams and are progressing through the plan, then make a change, this will be difficult for the Collaborator. Their challenge is that now they must start all over again gathering information from everyone and "taking care of" everyone else as they go through the revamp.

WHAT TO DO IF YOU ARE A COLLABORATOR

To help yourself understand and cope with change:

Use positive networking. As you gather information from others, carefully choose what questions you ask them. Choose questions that focus on the positive outcomes: "What benefits do you think we will get from going into teams?" "What are the possibilities for producing a better product (creating a better work environment, having more say, etc)?" You will help others, as well as yourself, advance toward the goal.

Volunteer for the planning subteam. Use your strength of knowing who is best for what function, by volunteering to be on the planning sub-team.

Combine ideas. Another of your strengths is being able to listen to others' ideas, then combine them to come up with an even better solution. Use this strength in your team meetings. It will help you and support your teammates.

Seek testimonials. Hearing how others have done it will help to make you feel more comfortable with teams.

Test: "Is this fact or opinion?" Because you are so open to information from others, you have a tendency to accept as fact what others say. Instead, add this sentence to your continual thought process, "Is this fact or opinion?" Adding a little of the Realist's skepticism will help to balance you out.

TECHNIQUES TO HELP YOUR COLLABORATOR TEAMMATES
How can you use the Collaborator's traits in a positive way?

Have informative meetings. The great thing about an informative meeting is you have everyone together at once, so everyone receives the same information. It helps eliminate the need for the gossip mill. As much as possible, be above board on information sharing.

Use their planning skills. Tap into their ability to know the skills of your teammates. Ask them to help with the planning.

Use testimonials. Because others' opinions and experiences are so important to Collaborators, they want to know what other groups have used teams. They like testimonials. It will make them feel more comfortable to talk to other successful people who've been through a similar experience.

Talk them through it. Allow extra time to talk the Collaborator through the use of teams. Talking is the way a Collaborator thinks things through.

The Goal Seeker

The Plusses + +

Goal Seekers accept change more quickly than the previous two styles, as long as it is presented appropriately. As their label foretells, you give them a goal, and they go for it. Whatever task they agree to do, they get it done. They are action-focused. They're also very good at cutting through red tape. If you have a meeting with a Collaborator, a Realist and a Goal Seeker, the Collaborator and Realist will creates many steps to get to the goal. The Goal Seeker will respond with, "Why do we need to have so many meetings and reports and authorizations? Let's just get it done!" This thought process can balance out the others.

The Minuses – –

Once given the goal, Goal Seekers can be very rigid about it. They get their sights set on that carrot at the end of the path, and they will take any shortcut or walk over anyone else to make sure they get the carrot. It's that challenge that gets their adrenaline going.

When the team is discussing any topic and the Goal Seeker has a specific idea about how to implement it, he or she may tend to discount others' ideas. Often they will send verbal "darts" or insults in response to others' ideas. This causes conflict and shuts down teammates' willingness to offer their own thoughts.

Realists are information focused, Collaborators are "other" focused and Goal Seekers are self-focused. They are focused on what is the benefit to them and how can it help their survival or thriving.

WHAT TO DO IF YOU ARE A GOAL SEEKER

The main advice to you centers around mental and verbal self-discipline:

Don't discount others. Yes, your idea is a good one and it is important to realize that other people may also have good ideas. When you are sarcastic to others, it hurts your relationship. On a team, we must all be interdependent. How would you feel if your teammates were not there at a time when you needed them? Temper your reactions to others' ideas.

Be open to multiple solutions/options. Because you are in such a hurry to get things done, you may have the tendency to take the first good idea and run with it. With the complexity of today's decisions and situations, we need all the good ideas we can get. Often it is a mix of several ideas that brings the best overall benefit. Please be patient and open.

When feeling rebellious, seek alternatives. When your patience wears thin due to others who require that specific procedures or steps must be followed, seek a way to do something "your way." Investigate, with your team or executives, the possibility of allowing you to do something that is important to you in your own way. When you are feeling angry because you've been "told" to do something, talk it out (calmly) with the other person. Sometimes even doing some physical exercise can get rid of your tension and help you relax.

Techniques to Help Your Goal Seeker Teammates

How can you use the Goal Seeker's traits in a positive way?

Focus on the goals and the gains. When introducing a change to a Goal Seeker, immediately address "What are you going to get out of it?" Goal Seekers tune in to the radio station WIIFM (What's In It For Me). Tap into their own sense of survival by focusing on what the goals and gains are for the Goal Seeker and the team. For example, "In 6 months' time, after we have met this goal, we will get a bonus!" Or, "After we have met this productivity level, we will receive an award!" Recognition is very important to a Goal Seeker. So at the end of the goal, any group recognition, or any form of recognition, is something they would look forward to.

Be quick and concise. Goal Seekers seem to always be in a hurry. When discussing a change to the team environment, they will feel most comfortable if the discussion is short and to the point.

Provide alternatives. When possible, allow team members a variety of ways to meet their part of the goal. The Realist will want specific, delineated steps, whereas the Goal Seeker will want some say in how the work is to be done.

Give them space to do it their way. Goal Seekers will take much more ownership and have more buy-in to the change when they can do at least part of it "their way."

Create an open, supportive communication environment. Make sure your Communication Guidelines prohibit sending verbal darts or sarcasm when ideas are being presented. The Negativity Bombardment Tool (see Lesson #7) is a great way to handle this issue.

The Visionary

The Plusses + +

This is your idea person. When change is introduced, a typical reaction from a Visionary is, "Wow! That's a terrific idea! Well, how about if we were to do it this way! Or this way! Or . . . " They will come up with 52 different ideas on how you could possibly do it. They accept change the most easily of any of these styles. For Visionaries, change is exciting and stimulating. It is their enthusiasm for new ideas that gives them the ability to enlist others' support and get them excited about the new way. They get people motivated and out of any negative slumps. Their enthusiasm is very contagious.

Visionaries are usually high risk-takers who like high stakes. They don't mind going forward without having all of the details outlined. The executive director of a national association, a Visionary, led the fight to file suit against the government. It was a big wager. A Realist would say, "Let's just gather information and see if we can present a case." In contrast, the Visionary says, "Let's go for it! This will be great! There's no time to waste."

The Minuses – –

Because Visionaries are "big picture" people, they are not as interested in the details. This also means they tend to be poor implementors. If they have to take care of many details, they will become frustrated quickly. It requires much more discipline for them to complete projects, than it does for the other three styles. Visionaries are good at starting projects, but may lose interest in them soon. In order to be effective, they usually surround themselves with other people who take care of the details or follow through.

Yes, Visionaries come up with many ideas, but some of them will be totally outrageous or infeasible. They may get very excited about a "half-baked" idea. A Realist may react with, "We don't have that kind of money!" Also a Visionary's idea of how much can be accomplished in a certain time period is often unrealistic.

Because Visionaries get bored quickly, they tend to reorganize frequently, rearranging their office or work space, moving furniture or changing work flow. Anything to make a change because they feel they get stagnant. If they can't change things in their area, they seek other ways to change things, which can cause problems for other people.

While working for Control Data, the author realized it was a company with a plethora of Visionaries in upper management. We were reorganized so frequently that the common joke was, "Who's my boss today? Where do I sit now?" We imagined these Visionaries staring at the organizational charts up on the wall, and getting bored with the arrangement — then just rearranging the boxes on the chart and feeling that this new way would enable us to perform better. They didn't understand what it meant to us out in the field, trying to continually deal with different managers, different territories or different product lines.

What To Do If You are a Visionary

These suggestions focus on achieving balance.

Ask yourself, "What is realistic?" Keep on producing your wonderful ideas, then consider "What is realistic?" Be open to the limitations of the real world. Yes, you may be better than anyone at coming up with ways to overcome obstacles or limitations. Keep your enthusiasm, while balancing it with realism.

Be patient. Remember, others need time and details to get ready to try something new.

Focus on short-term deadlines. By focusing on the short term, you can keep yourself motivated to continue to move through the implementation of a project. Keep one eye on the end vision and the other on the deadlines.

Techniques to Help Your Visionary Teammates

How can you use the Visionary's traits in a positive way?

Speak in big-picture terms. When you want a Visionary to buy into a new idea or a new way of doing things, speak of the big picture — the whole *Gestalt*. There is no need to immediately read to them all the proof and evidence of your point. Describe your idea in their language: "Imagine what it would be like in 12 months if we worked as a team." "Picture this!" "Visualize this! "Imagine . . . " and "What if . . . ?" are phrases that stimulate and excite a Visionary.

Share great ideas. If you want to bond with a Visionary and learn to look at the world from their perspective, sit around and share great ideas with them. Play the intellectual game of "What if . . . ?" "What if we had no financial limitations? What would we do differently?" You will both have a good time. This is also a good exercise to help Realists expand their perspective.

Be enthusiastic. When presenting a new idea to a Visionary, have enthusiasm in your voice. Be really convinced that this idea has great potential.

Use Visionaries to enlist others. You may want to take them aside before you introduce the idea to others. You could say, "I've got this really great idea. I bet you'll like it too. Picture this: in one year we will have a team that can . . . " When they are excited about it too, they will help champion the idea when it is shared with the rest of the team. This can help other team members get over their initial negativity to anything new or different.

Keep Visionaries on track. Because they have a hard time with details and long term implementation, devise ways to remind them and keep them focused on the deadlines. This will prevent the surprises on the deadline date, such as "Oh, man, I didn't get a chance to do that. I was so busy doing all these great ideas over here and great ideas over there, I never got around to finishing it." Having short-term goals helps everyone to stay focused and on target. Keep in mind that no one likes to be nagged or have someone else looking over their shoulder. Visionaries will feel very crowded if someone is continually reminding them of the details and deadlines. So be very creative and supportive in the ways you work with them. You can weave it into the conversation. If you are eating lunch with them, express your excitement about their part of the project. Then you will probably get a report on how they are doing with it, as well as the satisfaction of helping them refocus and get reignited about the work.

In Summary

In order to progress through the change into teams, it is very helpful to understand your own and your teammates' Change Styles.

Realists are very focused on information. Others may be annoyed by their continual questioning and negativity.

Collaborators are "people" persons who are good at involving everyone on the team. However, they may fuel the gossip mill during the transition period, and they tend to create bureaucracy (many meetings and authorizations) when facing the unknown.

Goal Seekers will make sure the team reaches the goal. Due to their laser focus on the goal, however, they may trample over the feelings of others and not listen to their input.

Visionaries are great at coming up with lots of ideas, and they have a positive, "We can do it!" attitude. Others may find it bothersome that the Visionary's ideas are often not thought out, and that they lack attention to detail and task completion.

Did you find yourself in any of these profiles? Did you see any of your teammates in them?

The techniques offered in this segment are meant to help everyone work with their strengths and gain support to adapt through their areas of less strength.

To function well as a team, each member must:

- Communicate with everyone who is related to the work, whether they are in or outside the department
- Focus more on the "we" than the "me"
- Focus more on "we can" do this, rather than "we can't"
- Learn how to reach consensus
- Have support to grow and glow
- Accept that there are multiple right answers (not just their own)
- Learn to listen as much as they talk
- Be patient with themselves and others
- Seek to understand before being understood

Another key is to remember that information, information, information helps almost everyone adapt to a new way of doing things. The more people feel out of the information loop, the more defensive and insecure they will feel, no matter what change style they are functioning from. By paying attention to how the people are adapting, and taking steps to support and aid those who need it, the transition will be easier for everyone. As people get used to more and more change, they can learn to flex to whatever style is needed to address the situation.

Louis V. Gerstner Jr., Chairman and CEO of IBM, has led that company out of a dangerous downward spiral. He says the way he has done it is to create an environment of "restless self-renewal." That means constant re-evaluation and change. His is a good example of what it takes to survive and thrive in the Knowledge Age: quick adaptability — a readiness to do things differently on short notice.

NOTES

1. J. A. Brimson and J. Antos, *Activity-Based Management For Service Industries, Government Entities, and Nonprofit Organizations* (New York: John Wiley & Sons, 1994).
2. Carl E. Larson and Frank M. J. LaFasto, *Teamwork, What Must Go Right/What Can Go Wrong* (Newbury Park, CA: Sage Publications, 1989) 33–34.
3. Adapted from B.W. Tuckerman, "Developmental sequence in small groups." *Psychological Bulletin* 63 (1965): (6):384–99.

Lesson #3

Choose the Right Type of Team

★ Virtual Teams

★ Spontaneous Teams

★ Reactive and Proactive Solution Teams

★ Venture Teams

★ Project Teams

★ Work Unit Teams

★ Cross-Functional Teams

★ Self-Directed Teams

Stage II:
Planning And Designing A Star Team^{SM} Culture

*M*oving from the Information Age to the Knowledge Age has brought about an evolution and growth of different types of teams, and the lesson that teams are not all created equal. The old philosophy that "a team is a team is a team" (that is, teams are generic), has gone by the wayside. Star Teams℠ come in different colors and shapes — in other words, they have different purposes and structures. Recognizing these differences and planning appropriately is what sets a team up for success. Here are some of the most common types of teams in the late 1990's:

> Virtual Teams
> Spontaneous Teams
> Proactive/Reactive Teams
> Creative/Venture Teams
> Project Teams
> Work Unit Teams
> Cross-Functional Teams
> Self-Directed Teams

Choosing the right types of teams for your situation is an essential element in implementing the Process and People aspects of shifting to a team-based culture and establishing your Star Teams℠.

Each Star Team℠ type requires its own unique focus, process and way of relating. You must pass through two levels to make this process useful: the first is to understand these differences so you can construct the team accordingly. The second (and more challenging) one is for each member to actually "be" different on each team, according to what is needed. This requires flexibility, discipline and personal focus. Team players may need instruction and coaching when they are working on a new type of team. It is actually stimulating and expanding for people to use different parts of their capabilities. Setting each team player up with the appropriate structure, training and coaching brings out each one's star potential.

It is interesting to note that no matter what the team type, people still have a basic need for structure. Adding definition for their new roles helps them adjust and adapt.

How to Use this Lesson

To help you design and work successfully in each type of team, this comprehensive lesson offers a description of each team, plus a look at the process as well as the people aspects involved. Team sections are divided into the following subsections:

- The Process Dynamics: How to set up the structure and operation unique to this team type.
- Meeting Dynamics: The most effective meeting flow for successful team function.
- The People Dynamics: How the four change styles will likely react and perform within this team.
- Star Tips: Essentials for ensuring team effectiveness.

Virtual Teams

Refers to teams whose members are not physically located close to each other, or who may work on different shifts. They may be spread throughout a building, a city, the country or in multiple countries. Members may be home-based, working at different offices, or on the road.

Virtual teams that are Star Teams℠ strategically use modern technology to overcome time and distance differences, improve communications, and make better use of the team's brain trust. But knowing when to use technology vs. face-to-face meetings is also a strategic decision.

The Process Dynamics

Initial coalescing is crucial for any virtual team. Because of distance or alternate shift challenges, communications becomes the biggest issue. To assure success (good communications, high trust, everyone going in the same direction), people in virtual teams need to be face-to-face at the beginning of the development of the team. If they are brand new to teaming, they should go through their training together.

Every Star Virtual Team should meet to agree on its:

- Communication guidelines (see Lesson 7)
- Communication systems (i.e., what media, what information to share and how/when response is expected)
- Decision-making (when independent and when team decision)
- Goal(s)
- Implementation plan

It is important to document and circulate all agreements. This initial time should also be used to get to know each other's communication and contribution styles, as well as come to consensus on goals and process. Then team members can go in their various directions to implement the plan.

Frequent communication is important for virtual teams. Communication system agreements should include at least weekly checking in or reporting, whether on e-mail, voice mail, fax, telephone/video conference or any other media. One essential effectiveness tool for a virtual team is to make sure members get together in a face-to-face meeting **at least twice** a year.

MEETING DYNAMICS

The first meeting should begin informally with planned interactions to get to know each other as people (not just functions). When addressing the communication guidelines and systems, decision-making, goals and implementation plan, someone who is a good facilitator should lead the meeting. The facilitator does not necessarily have to be part of the team.

USE OF ELECTRONIC MEDIA

> "For virtual teams, processing leaps across space, time and organization boundaries. Data flows to and from and among many different locations."[1]

Each virtual team needs to think through what technology is most helpful in meeting team goals. One way to do this is to have each member complete an Electronic Communication Availability form, such as the

Electronic Communication Availability			
	Available	**Preferred**	**Address**
Phone			
Voice Mail			
E-mail			
Fax			
Teleconference			
Videoconference			
PC conference			
Groupware*			
Software types			

---

*Often groupware companies will offer training in using their medium as a teaming tool, helping each team member adapt to this tool.

example shown, indicating availability of and preference for various media.

In research conducted on Geographically Dispersed Teams (GDT's), Sonya Prestridge of the Center for Creative Leadership discovered that GDT's mainly use face-to-face communications and e-mail to exchange critical business information and maintain social contact. Problems were encountered with other electronic communications due to team members not being trained in their use and everyone not having the same type of medium.[2]

To ensure success, have specific times to meet, whether on-line or via video or teleconference. Produce and distribute an agenda ahead of time. Assure all handouts get to each member in a reasonable amount of time to read before the meeting.

VIRTUAL PLACES

"Creating virtual places is initially about making adequate substitutes for physical places."[3] The "virtual place" may be an online discussion area only accessible by the team, often called a "team room." In *No Sense of Place*, Joshua Meyrowitz says that due to extensive use of technology, the need for a tie between a physical and social place is dissolved.

The People Dynamics

Team members who are spread apart often feel alone, unrecognized, "out of the loop." Additionally, they may end up going off in their own direction, losing track of the team direction due to lack of contact. Self-discipline and a comfort with using technology for communications are important characteristics of Virtual Team members. Knowing how to help each team member adapt and stay on track is vital on a virtual team.

HOW THE CHANGE STYLES ADAPT

Think of the people you have or plan to have on your team. Consider the four different styles people use to adapt to change (described in Lesson #2). Which of these is the more dominant style for each one of your existing or proposed team members? The following insights will help you anticipate what reactions you might have from each person to participating on a Virtual Team.

Realists will usually love working alone. Watch out for over-researching or going off on tangents.

Collaborators will really miss being with people. Arrange as frequent contact as possible, especially with voice, video teleconference or face to face.

Goal Seekers can often function well on their own. However, they will need recognition for their progress on a regular basis.

People Focused Visionaries need the stimulus of conversation. They can often handle communications via any media, electronic or otherwise. **Individualist Visionaries** may have a hard time communicating their great ideas and where they are going with them to the rest of the team. The challenge with all visionaries is to keep them on track because they are easily distracted and often go off on tangents.

COMMUNICATIONS

Because there is no way to see body language or tell the difference in tone of voice, it becomes even more important to check for understanding of e-mail or written communications. It is amazing how the same words can mean totally different things to different people, as in these examples:

"What more do you want me to do?" could mean a sincere inquiry for more work. It could also be expressed with an emphasis on "more," which could mean a grudge is held and sarcasm is meant.

"You want to check my answers?" could be an invitation to check my answers. Or, a defensive, alarmed reaction actually communicating: "I can't believe you don't trust me."

Virtual teams have their socialization needs, just as do face-to-face (co-located) teams. But it takes a bit longer for them to build their communication patterns and establish trust. The communication guidelines mentioned in Lesson #7 also apply here. It helps to begin each meeting with some small talk to re-establish the relationships. It is human nature to listen better and to be more willing to cooperate with someone to whom you feel bonded.

In the Center for Creative Leadership's study of Geographically Dispersed Teams, it was learned that GDT's spent 20.6% of their face-to-face meeting time in relationship building and 77.7% devoted to business or task work. The majority (65%) meet for two or more days. This longer meeting time is important for GDT's because they see each other less frequently. The focus on relationship building becomes more critical when face-to-face meetings are infrequent.

Information becomes the medium for socialization, as discussed by Joshua Meyrowitz in *No Sense of Place*. Sharing information provides a sense of belonging and bonding. Trust may be built or destroyed by how teammates respond to the shared information.[4]

Suggestion

For most important points, be sure to:
- Say them several different ways
- Give an example
- Use a metaphor. Example: "oval like a football"
- Ask others to translate what things mean to them. Example: "Given that this is the goal, how would you implement it?"

ACKNOWLEDGE CONCERNS

The Center for Creative Leadership's study revealed that conflicts going unidentified and taking longer to address were a key challenge for GDT's. Sharing concerns helps to keep communication lines open. Sharing a concern early can prevent a grudge from being built over time. Often bringing up the concern can correct a misunderstanding and prevent a conflict. Remember to express the concern with tact and be open to listening to responses from others.

Even if the concern has no apparent impact on the team, sharing it may still be helpful. An example is a teammate concerned about having to let go of a key employee. Once shared, the concerned teammate may benefit from the team's expression of understanding or advice.

SELF-DISCIPLINE

Virtual team members must be more self-disciplined than other team types because teammates are not around to remind each other to stay focused. The issue of "Is everyone pulling their load?" is very common in virtual teams due to less frequent communications and lack of visibility. It is important for virtual team members to check in frequently using their agreed-upon technology/communications mechanisms. That may mean checking voice mail or e-mail hourly. Star Virtual Team players seek to understand each other, stay in close communication and have a high level of self-discipline.

" . . . heed what we have heard repeatedly from our on-the-ground virtual team experts: "It's 90 percent people and 10 percent technology."[5]

☆ **Tip for Effective Virtual Teams**

    ☆ One essential effectiveness tool for a virtual team is to make sure its members get together in a face-to-face meeting at least twice a year.

Spontaneous Teams

"Let's get the key people together this afternoon to solve this issue." In today's business world there is no time to waste. Fast response can make the difference between survival and demise in the new millennium.

Spontaneous Teams are:

- Necessary when time is short
- Usually project or issue based
- Short term

Case

When IBM came to Microsoft with a partnership contract regarding designing an operating system, Microsoft's key people quickly convened to discuss it and said they would sign it right away.

    When IBM went to Intergalactic Digital Research (at the time, a better known company than Microsoft), an executive at Digital said they needed time to consider it and to run it past their attorneys, who dragged their feet. IBM observed Digital's sluggish response and decided to risk using a lesser known company who was more responsive. Thus began the stellar rise of Microsoft.

The Process Dynamics

Many businesses tell me they have many Spontaneous Teams. In reality, they have spontaneous groups, not teams. Being able to have and participate in a Spontaneous Team requires some of the highest level teaming abilities of any of the team types, with the exception of self-directed teams. Because time is of the essence in a Spontaneous Team, roles, communication guidelines and decision-making authority need to be established and agreed upon quickly. We recommend a Spontaneous Team have only one goal. Spontaneous Teams work best when the teammates have worked together before on another type of team.

MEETING DYNAMICS

Calling these teams "Spontaneous" does not mean there is no planning or forethought to their meetings. In order to get the most out of the short time available, a concise, goal-focused agenda should be used. Participants should quickly assess everyone's roles and expected contributions, and then proceed.

The People Dynamics

Being able to collaborate quickly is a vital skill in the new millennium. It often requires the ability to:

- Switch focus quickly
- Think well on your feet
- Quickly assess which of your skills are needed — based on what the situation requires and what skills others on the team have or don't have
- Leave personality issues outside the door
- Make decisions with less information available
- Work well with people from different disciplines

HOW THE CHANGE STYLES ADAPT

Think of the people you have or plan to have on your team. Consider the four different styles people use to adapt to change (described in Lesson #2). Which of these is the more dominant style for each one of your existing or proposed team members? The following insights will help you anticipate what reactions you might have from each person to participating on a Spontaneous Team.

Realists may struggle with being on a Spontaneous Team because the speed necessitates less research and less time to gather information. They will feel uncomfortable making decisions without this information. However, they serve a very important function on Spontaneous Teams, by helping to balance out the sense of urgency with emphasis on thinking it through and planning it well.

Collaborators may feel a struggle with Spontaneous Teams due to their need for a lot of discussion on an issue. In a Spontaneous Team, time is often short, so discussions will need to be concise. In addition, they often feel insecure making a decision that others may disagree with. If Collaborators have a personality issue with someone on the team, they will often "shut down" and not participate much. They do this because they realize there is no time to resolve the issue, so they prefer not to deal with it. They shut down in order to hold it within. However, Collaborators will help the Spontaneous Team assess what skills are needed and what team members have them, and help the team create a supportive atmosphere amidst a sense of chaos.

Goal Seekers love Spontaneous Teams because they appeal to their sense of urgency and quick accomplishment. However, watch out for their need to use the first good idea, jump to a conclusion or not think things through well enough. Having both a Realist and Goal Seeker on the Spontaneous Team can balance this out.

Visionaries like Spontaneous Teams because they are comfortable with making decisions without enough information. They also like the adrenalin effect of a spontaneous meeting. Visionaries also need the Realist, in this case, to balance out their tendency to have "pie in the sky" ideas.

Star Spontaneous Teams have high level abilities in fast thinking, flexibility, decision-making and ego-less collaboration.

☆ **Tips for Effective Spontaneous Teams**
Being able to collaborate quickly is an important skill. Key requirements are the ability to:

☆ switch focus quickly
☆ think well on your feet
☆ quickly assess which skills are needed
☆ leave personality issues outside the door
☆ make decisions with incomplete information available
☆ involve people from different departments or disciplines

Reactive and Proactive Solution Teams

The world that we have made as a result of the level of thinking we have done thus far, creates problems that we cannot solve at the same level at which we created them."
—Albert Einstein

Not only are the old ways of solving problems not working anymore, but there are now problems that have never been seen before. This requires a different approach, which is why we advocate the use of Reactive and Proactive Solution Teams.

Some would call these teams problem prevention or problem solving teams. We believe it is wasteful of energy to focus on the negative: i.e., "the problem." A negative focus causes defensiveness and a downward spiral of mental energy. Americans have been well known as good problem solvers. However this has kept us from being able to think beyond the problem — in other words, outside the box. More creative thought is needed in the third millennium. By focusing on potential solutions and actions, creative juices begin to flow.

Reactive Teams: The Process Dynamics

The Reactive Team is a more familiar commodity/structure since the traditional hierarchical structure is focused on problem solving. Some corporations are so problem focused that they have assigned full-time people whose job is to find problems around the company and solve them. One of these people came to an Enlightened Leadership Institute (ELI) workshop, which focuses on the positive, solution side. He walked out halfway through the workshop, saying that if he followed what ELI was advocating, he would be out of a job.

The hierarchical business structure is based on a problem solving focus:

Traditional Approach to Problem Solving

Step 1: Identify the problem [look for the cause(s) and who's to blame]
Step 2: Manager decides on the solution
Step 3: Manager tells everyone what they need to do differently
Step 4: Overcome all the resistance caused by Steps 1, 2 and especially 3.

Meeting Dynamics

In the new millennium, we look at what we traditionally called "problems" more in terms of an exciting challenge or opportunity. In the 1990's, business gave this perspective "lip service," but in the new millennium it will become the standard. If something breaks down, it is an opportunity to look at it fresh to see if there is a better way to reconstruct it so it won't break down again. To create positive, solution focused environment, the questions in the "Solution Focus" can be used as the agenda.

The Solution Focus

(adapted from Enlightened Leadership International, Inc.'s "Framework" technique[6])

What, specifically, are we doing that is working?
What is our objective?
What could we do **differently** that would get us closer to our goal?
What could we do **better** that would get us closer to our goal?
What could we do **more of** that would get us closer to our goal?

For those who are concerned that we are not addressing "the problem," look closer at these two questions: What could we do **differently** that would get us closer to our goal? What could we do **better** that would get us closer to our goal? These questions shift the focus from the negative side of the issue. The result is more creativity and better solutions.

THE CAUSE

You may be concerned that we are not addressing the cause of the problem. Think of discussions or meetings you've had where "the cause" was discussed. What was it like? Were people defensive, in essence saying, "I'm not to blame"? Were fingers pointed at each other to make others "responsible" for the problem?

If the problem is technical related, it is easier for objectivity to reign supreme. But the minute the human element is involved, barriers go up. If you feel an absolute necessity to discuss the cause, take every measure you can to keep the discussion objective, looking to the factors of the circumstance and not laying blame.

Reactive Teams: The People Dynamics

Q: What happens to people's energy level and focus when discussing "What have we been doing that is working?"

A: Energy is high! Usually everyone is chiming in with ideas about what is going right. The reason for the qualifier "usually" is that for teams that are negative focused, it may feel awkward and unsafe to talk about what is working. Once a positive and supportive environment is created, team members will excitedly list what went right. Bringing this high energy level into the upcoming discussion of the objective keeps everyone's enthusiasm and focus high on this important subject.

Q. What happens to people's energy level and focus when discussing "the objective"?

A: You may notice that "What is our objective?" is the second question, not the first. Enlightened Leadership (and this author) have observed that many people's energy, enthusiasm and focus "tune out" when discussing the objective. But the objective is very important. Staying focused on and continually clarifying the objective:

- Keeps team members going in the same direction both during and outside of meetings.
- Helps team members think through their contribution to the goal.
- Provides a measure at the end to see progress, thus providing the reason to celebrate.

Discussing the objective after the past successes promotes an attitude of "we're on our way!" This simultaneously keeps energy high and focus on the objective. Star Reactive Team members need to have a positive, "we can do it!" attitude. The team may be required to deal with challenges they have no experience with, function with fewer resources than they need, or deal with a customer's anger while solving the problem. The member needs to be both a thinker and action focused.

How the Change Styles Adapt

Think of the people you have or plan to have on your team. Consider the four different styles people use to adapt to change (described in Lesson #2). Which of these is the more dominant style for each one of your existing or proposed team members? The following insights will help you anticipate what reactions you might have from each person to participating on a Reactive Team.

Realists love the basic idea for a Reactive Team because they love to solve problems. This brings up the frustration they will have on Reactive Teams — they want to approach the issue from the problem, not the solution perspective. A full explanation of the Solution Focus and practice using it will make the Realists more comfortable and help them make the transition.

Collaborators tend to feel very comfortable with the Solution Focus because they like to focus on the positive (avoiding conflict). One exception is the Collaborator type that is a whiner. They may tend to want to focus on the cause of the problem, especially if it is perceived to be caused by someone not on the team.

Goal Seekers will also feel very comfortable with Reactive Teams because of their need to overcome challenges ("climb the mountain"). However, as in the Spontaneous Teams situation, watch out for their need to use the first good idea, jump to a conclusion or not think things through well enough. Again, having both a Realist and Goal Seeker on the team can balance this out.

Visionaries are solution focused by nature. Use their positive focus and enthusiasm to keep everyone else focused on the solution. They will probably come up with many ideas for solutions.

Star Reactive Teams focus more on the solution than on who or what is to blame for the problem. The results are quicker, more creative on-target solutions, with Star Team℠ members feeling invigorated to implement the solution.

☆ **Tip for Effective Reactive Teams**

    ☆ Reactive team effectiveness is increased if the four-step Solution Focus process is followed.

Proactive Teams: The Process Dynamics

Problem prevention teams, or Proactive Teams, used to be regarded with an attitude of, "Yeah, it would be nice to have time to have Proactive Teams, but we are too busy reacting to the problems at hand to think about preventing any!" In the new millennium, many companies are learning that Proactive Teams (next to Venture Teams) are a valuable competitive edge that can assure a strong future.

So what does a Proactive Team do? How does one work? In most cases, the objectives of a Proactive Team are to **anticipate problems/ challenges** that might happen, and design and oversee implementation of a new strategy or solution.

MEETING DYNAMICS

The process is to combine analytical research with creative and foresightful thinking, in a free flowing yet productive interplay. When creativity is being tapped, the meeting structure should be informal and open. Often the analytical research is done outside the meeting, but presented during the meeting. More structure is needed for the analytical segment.

The Analytical Side — Factfind

Be clear on the goal to be addressed. Gather the facts, statistics, competitive information, internal and industry-wide trends or any other relevant information.

The Creative Side — Brainstorm

Use the brainstorming guidelines described in the Venture Teams section to come up with a list of possible obstacles or opportunities that may arise.

The Analytical Side Again — Strategize

Look back at the lists of possibilities and compare to your goals and available resources. Address feasibility issues. Then design your strategy.

The Creative Side Again — Evaluate

After designing the strategy, ask these questions:

- Does this strategy make us unique or set us apart from others?
- Does it provide the competitive edge we need?
- Does it reach far enough?
- Does it inspire us?

If the answer is "No" to any of these questions, then ask, "What would it take to . . . " For example, "What would it take to create a strategy that inspires us?"

THE CONCLUSION

You will decide which, if any, of these questions are relevant or important to your situation. Based on the answers, it is up to your team to change or finalize your strategy. But be ready to change the plan, because flexibility is essential in order to shine in the new business environment.

The People Dynamics

Star Proactive Team members need to be able to switch quickly from analytical to creative functions. It also helps to have a macro as well as a micro point of view. They must also be able to drop their ego attachment to the ideas they have contributed, so they can stay open to consider everyone's ideas.

HOW THE STYLES ADAPT

Think of the people you have or plan to have on your team. Consider the four different styles people use to adapt to change (described in Part II: The People section of Lesson #2). Which of these is the more dominant style for each one of your existing or proposed team members? The following insights will help you anticipate what reactions you might have from each person to participating on a Proactive Team.

Realists will be most comfortable with analytical discussions. Make sure that you have a complement of Visionaries on the Proactive Team to assure balance.

Collaborators will have fun on the Proactive Team. They will help to bring together the analytical ideas of the Realists, as well as the creative ideas of the Visionaries.

Goal Seekers may have an approach/avoidance reaction to the Proactive Team. Because they love to be competitive and prepared, they will be attracted to those features of the team's purpose. However, they may feel frustrated by the time required to brainstorm the possibilities. Also, remember that Goal Seekers may tend to shoot down others' ideas, so use the Negativity Bombardment Tool (see Lesson #7) for these discussions.

Visionaries are essential to have on the Proactive Team because their strengths will be put to good use on the creative aspects of this process. Be sure to set up an environment of fun for the creative discussions.

☆ **Tips for Effective Proactive Teams**

- ☆ They may only need to meet once or a few times.
- ☆ It's helpful to have a mixture of newer and more senior people on the team, as well as people from different disciplines.
- ☆ It can also be helpful to have a user or customer on the team if possible.

The use of Star Proactive Teams can be an important competitive edge to help the organization be prepared for what could have been a challenging surprise.

Venture Teams

Looking beyond old approaches is critical for millennium competitiveness and survival. In Venture Teams, minds come together to **anticipate future needs** of the customer, company, or employees. These could involve new products, markets or joint ventures; new ways to organize the company; or new roles or services for the employees. It is important to maintain a strong focus on both the company's goal and the team's goal throughout the team's process.

The Process Dynamics

Venture Teams require high level collaborative creativity. In order to assure productivity, the environment must support this process.

MEETING DYNAMICS

The Creative Phase is more informal and open, with a "fun" atmosphere. The Strategic Phase is formal with a more analytical focus.

THE CREATIVE PHASE

A very special mindset and communication environment is necessary for Venture Teams to be productive. We have learned much from the computer industry about how to promote "out of the box" thinking. They create environments that support revolutionary thinking.

The foundation of this environment is support for open communications. The "Team Communications Guidelines" discussed in Lesson #7 need to be used in order to assure open communications. They are listed here for your convenience.

Team Communication Guidelines

❏ Really Listen: Don't "Wait to Talk"
When others are speaking, focus on what they are saying, trying to understand their meaning completely. Don't be focusing on what you are going to be saying next.

❏ Be Concise
For those who are outgoing and talkative, be concise, get to the point and do not monopolize the conversation. Give everyone in the group the chance to shine.

❏ Speak Up
If you are quieter or shy, speak up and share your ideas and questions. Others can benefit from your participation.

❏ Be Open-Minded
Reserve judgments. Consider all points of view and possibilities.

❏ Show Respect
Respect one another while talking or listening.

❏ Tell the Truth with Tact
Mom was right. "Honesty is the best policy." However, remember that tact should be used to assure the communication is really heard.

❏ Think Before Speaking
Put your brain in gear before taking your mouth out of "park."

❏ Avoid Derision or Sarcasm
Making fun of others can hurt communications.

❏ Seek and Confirm Understanding
When you are unsure of what someone means, ask for clarification. To confirm that you understand, summarize back to them what you heard.

❑ More Than One Right Answer
Appreciate the diversity on the team. Each person brings a different skill set and perspective. Accept that there can be more than one right way to solve a problem.

❑ Disagreement Is O.K., Conflict Is Not
Disagreement is intellectual, conflict is emotional.

❑ Additional Guidelines
What other agreements would be important in order to assure that **your team** maintains open communications?

BARNSTORMING BRAINSTORMING

Once an environment of open communications is established, minds will be more open to explore new thoughts. Since the Venture Team needs to project into the future, they need to use their creative thinking in a brainstorming way. To elevate the brainstorming process to its maximum level of effectiveness, use the following thoughts and actions:

+ Everyone participates
+ Know that there is more than one solution
+ Encourage thinking beyond the obvious and usual
+ Welcome outrageous ideas
+ Introduce more "play" when playing with ideas, e.g., toss balls or koosh balls
+ Build or "springboard" on each other's ideas to develop them further
+ Suspend assumptions
+ Play "What if . . . "
+ Listen to each other *(This is worth repeating)*
+ Avoid criticism *(This is also worth repeating)*
+ Laugh a lot
+ Change where you meet to a very different environment (one that is still supportive of what you must accomplish)
+ Let everyone have markers so they can write their own ideas on the flipchart paper (this avoids control issues by the scribe who may choose not to record ideas he/she does not like or agree with)

"Wisdom comes not from knowing the answers but in realizing how many questions remain."
— Richard Berendzen

CAN'T IS A FOUR LETTER WORD

When someone says "I/we can't do that," creative thinking is squashed. Often what is really meant is:

"I don't want to do that."
"Based on previous assumptions, we don't know how."
"We have not had permission in the past."
"We have not had the resources for doing that."
"I don't want to change from the current way because it is comfortable to me."

The purpose of creative thinking is to let go of past assumptions, rules and limitations, especially during the brainstorming phase. That is why there is such a strong emphasis on creating a non-judgmental environment that is supportive of all kinds of ideas.

MIXING IT UP

If a Venture team functions over a period of time, members may find it necessary to "mix it up a little" because they may become stale. For instance, a tire company was concerned about its recent lack of product innovation. Upon analyzing their R&D team, they realized the same people had been on the team for many years. They were stagnant. The company decided to move people in and out of the team on a more regular basis. This greatly improved the flow of new ideas and increased individual motivation.[7]

THE OUTSIDER'S VIEW

Another way to get a fresh perspective is to bring someone in from outside the company. Some good examples are:

• A customer or user of the product or service

Case

One of the instrumental changes in CHRYSLER'S approach which turned the company around was changing the design team from exclusively engineers. By adding a sales person, a car insurance company representative, and someone from manufacturing, they found they were able to cut many steps from the design process and create features that would reduce insurance costs and satisfy the customer more.

- A vendor or subcontractor who is involved in the product or service somewhere in its process

THE STRATEGIC PHASE

Some Venture Teams are simply charged with coming up with lists of possibilities, then passing it off to others to decide on feasibility and strategy. Whoever is responsible for this phase, know that the focus of this phase is strategic and analytical — the opposite of the Creative Phase.

Suggestion

If the results of the Creative Phase are passed to another team for the Strategic Phase, make sure some of the Creative Phase members are on the new team.

The purpose of the Strategic Phase is to decide which of the possibilities will be chosen as a strategy. Considerations of money, time and other resources must be addressed at this time. Even during this phase it is important not to squash ideas.

Case

Several computer companies wanted to create "mega-computers," but none had or wanted to spend the extensive R & D expense necessary. This could have put a stop to the research ideas due to lack of capital. But one of the company's executives thought outside the box and decided to invite his competition to join him in the venture. Together they formed a new venture company and all benefitted from the research.

The People Dynamics

Qualities to look for or build in members of a Venture team:

+ out-of-the-box thinking
+ a wide variety of points of view
+ open-mindedness
+ macro as well as micro point of view

As in the Proactive Team, Venture members must also be able to drop their ego attachment to the ideas they have contributed, so they can stay open to consider everyone's ideas.

HOW THE CHANGE STYLES ADAPT

Think of the people you have or plan to have on your team. Consider the four different styles people use to adapt to change (described in Part II: The People section of Lesson #2). Which of these is the more dominant style for each one of your existing or proposed team members? The following insights will help you anticipate what reactions you might have from each person to participating on a Venture Team.

Realists will probably struggle with being on the Creative Phase of this team due to the unstructured environment. But their strengths will be needed in the Strategic Phase.

Collaborators will enjoy the Creative Phase, helping to create a supportive communication environment. They will be fine contributors in the Strategic Phase, but may not enjoy it as much.

Goal Seekers, once loosened up, will enjoy and be good contributors to both phases of this team.

For **Visionaries,** being on a Venture Team is their dream come true. They will probably help get the rest of the team members to expand their thinking. They will also often fight hard for the ideas when they are being considered during the Strategic Phase.

☆ Tips for Effective Venture Teams

☆ Create a fun, supportive atmosphere for meetings.

☆ Rotate or change the team members to maintain a fresh perspective.

☆ Revisit the goal frequently (because getting off track can be easy on these teams).

☆ Post the goal boldly in the meeting room to help keep the team focused.

Star Venture Teams can catapult an organization ahead of its competitors by anticipating the customer, company or employee needs. Members of this type of team need to switch on their open communications, creativity and brainstorming skills.

Project Teams

Project teams are focused on a goal that has a specific time line. They have a clearcut beginning and end and a well defined expectation for results.

The Process Dynamics

MEETING DYNAMICS

The focus on a Project Team meeting is often on the entire process of design, development and implementation. Each person has a well defined role (related to their area of expertise), contributing toward the outcome of the project. The agenda is usually formal and progress is often charted.

A common challenge with project teams occurs about halfway through the implementation stage. Something happens that makes everyone aware that there are different interpretations of the goal of the project. To avoid this challenge:

* Spend time at the beginning to discuss what the goal really means to each person.
* Revisit the purpose on a regular basis, e.g., once per month on a six month project.
* Make the goal visible, e.g., typed at the top of each agenda.

The People Dynamics

Essential characteristics for members of a Project Team:

+ Focus
+ Knowledgeable on the subject
+ Good accountability for their responsibilities
+ Ability to think through a whole process
+ Ability to stay committed until the project is completed

HOW THE CHANGE STYLES ADAPT

Think of the people you have or plan to have on your team. Consider the four different styles people use to adapt to change (described in Part II: The People section of Lesson #2). Which of these is the more dominant style for each one of your existing or proposed team members? The following insights will help you anticipate what reactions you might have from each person to participating on a Project Team.

Realists will love being on a project team. They will be good at laying out the steps in the plan and keeping the rest of the team focused on what needs to be done. Their challenge will come if a change is required midstream or if the Goal Seeker suggests shortcuts. Thoroughly answering their questions and explaining the reasons for the change or shortcuts can help Realists adapt. Another tool to help the Realist is illustrated in this example:

Steve, a sales rep and Goal Seeker, heard from the client that an order needed to be delivered two months earlier than originally planned. When presenting this news to the team, he put it this way, "Our client has an opportunity to get a very large account if they can get our software two months earlier than planned. They are willing to pay us extra for the rush status. What are your ideas on how we can shorten our process in order to help the client out?"

Realists need to know *why* the change is occurring. They also respond well to a question or a request to help solve a problem. Approached in this way, they are more likely to respond favorably.

Collaborators will do well on a Project Team. They will help everyone bond and often can mediate conflicts. Some Collaborators, however, are fearful of conflicts and don't know how to mediate them, so they will want to sweep differences of opinion under the rug.

Goal Seekers love Project Teams because of the specific target and timeline. Goal Seekers need to have some say about how the project will be implemented in order to have buy-in.

Visionaries may be challenged by the need to maintain interest and focus throughout the project. Periodically revisit the picture of the project result to reinspire the Visionary. The more visible you can make the progress of the project, the more motivating it will be for both the Visionary and the Goal Seeker. Others may need to check on the status of the Visionary's part of the project because he or she may lose interest over time.

☆ Tips for Effective Project Teams

☆ Be very clear up front on the desired outcome of the project.

☆ Be sure to create a timeline chart with milestones in order to monitor progress.

☆ Take advantage of software programs available to help with project management.

Star Project Team members are carefully chosen for their subject matter expertise and ability to stay committed to the team until the project is complete.

Work Unit Teams

Work unit teams are made up of individuals who must rely on working together to produce the results expected for their department. Usually their functions are similar, e.g., the MIS Department. Some people call them functional teams. The challenge with "functional" is that it implies the opposite too, i.e. dysfunctional. The term Work Unit focuses on the task and the group of people in the section or unit. Additionally, "unit" is derived from "one." *The American College Dictionary* defines unit as an "undivided entity" — a good goal for a team.

The Process Dynamics

In the past, departments were run more as groups than as teams. Now, in the Knowledge Age, we are seeing higher productivity by showing the work unit how to work as a team. What's the difference?

At a typical work group meeting, people either listen to the department head provide information and instructions, or they each report on the status of their work. In a Work Unit Team, meeting leadership is often alternated. In addition, participants have other roles such as Scribe and Timekeeper (see Lesson #8 for roles). When status reports are given, Work Unit Team members not only listen, but carry the following questions in their minds:

- How can this relate to my responsibilities?
- Is there a way my work can interrelate with this person's?
- Can I do something in my work to build on what this person is doing?
- How can we help each other to advance our work?
- Do I have any ideas or suggestions that may help this person?

For the Work Unit Team, a review of Lesson #8 on "How to Prevent Toxic Team Meetings" will be very helpful in creating synergy.

Meeting Dynamics

Use a formal agenda which usually addresses status reports, unit focused problem solving and some planning.

The People Dynamics

Essential characteristics for members of a Work Unit Team:

+ Knowledge of their area
+ Willingness to help with the meeting process by serving in different roles such as Team Leader, Facilitator, Scribe or Timekeeper
+ Interest in helping others on the team

HOW THE CHANGE STYLES ADAPT

Think of the people you have or plan to have on your team. Consider the four different styles people use to adapt to change (described in Part II: The People section of Lesson #2). Which of these is the more dominant style for each one of your existing or proposed team members? The following insights will help you anticipate what reactions you might have from each person to participating on a Work Unit Team.

Realists will be very comfortable with most of a Work Unit Team's functioning. When it is their turn to lead or facilitate the meeting, they may feel intimidated by the task. The meetings they lead will probably be run very rigidly. They will prefer to be the Timekeeper or Scribe.

Collaborators will also be very comfortable with a Work Unit Team. Facilitating the meeting will be a good fit for the Collaborator. Timekeeper may be a challenge for them because they may hesitate to interrupt the flow of the meeting to tell people the time has run out.

Goal Seekers may be challenged when someone other than themselves, or the person who used to be the department head, is leading the meeting. Even though Goal Seekers hate to admit it, they like the authority structure of the hierarchy — the department head carried authority and thus respect. Patience with someone who is new to the function of Team Leader or Facilitator may be tough for the Goal Seeker. One way to increase their patience is to ask them to coach the Realist or Collaborator in preparation for their first time as Team Leader or Facilitator. Taking responsibility for helping another person can create a different level of understanding and patience for the Goal Seeker. A course in coaching would also be helpful.

Visionaries will like the variety that comes from different leaders and people assuming different roles. A stimulating assignment for the Visionary is to come up with a Meeting Opener for many of the meetings.

☆ Tips for Effective Work Unit Teams

☆ Work to create synergy and high levels of trust and respect (training in listening and trust building can help with this).

☆ Seek to understand the interdependency of each team member.

☆ Get to know each other as "whole people" — not just for the function each person provides.

Star Work Unit Team members focus on their interdependency in order to create a synergy that results in more productivity and a greater sense of team bonding.

Cross-Functional Teams

A Cross-Functional Team is made up of members who are from other teams or departments. The term implies different disciplines, but does not require it. For example, two teams that run similar machinery may need to combine parts of their teams in order to coordinate production or use of the same resources. The combined group is a Cross-Functional Team because there are representatives from two different teams. Another example is an executive team which would commonly include the Team Leaders from marketing, operations, information technology and manufacturing. Cross-Functional Teams require a different approach because there is a higher chance of:

- Different points of view
- Different "agendas" or goals
- Territoriality

The Process Dynamics

Cross-Functional Teams are used for a variety of purposes. Dennen Steel uses them in two situations:

1. Problems Between Teams/Departments

Dennen's main teams are Work Unit Teams focused around what used to be departments. On their Cross-Functional Teams, representatives from each team form a new team to address an area of concern. The beauty of this approach is that they do not have to shut down production to have a meeting. Additionally, they are given the right to invite any one else who may be critical to solving the problem. The lifespan of these teams is often dependent on the resolution of the problem.

2. Cross Team Interdependency

Dennen also uses Cross-Functional Teams when a functional area has frequent interface with other areas. This necessity was discovered after a newly-formed Work Unit Team was having a hard time meeting its own goals because of its interdependency with another team's work. The two teams had called themselves "The Steel Hogs" and "The Cutting Edge." Since the prime function of both teams was to slit coil, they shared people back and forth depending on orders. As team members were discussing the impact of other groups on their success, they also decided to include sales, production control and finance. The new Cross-Functional Team called itself "The Slit Coil Team."

MEETING DYNAMICS

To assure that the focus stays on the team goal and not on individual agendas, discuss and define the goal at the beginning. Then have each person describe what the goal means for his or her area and how they see it benefitting the Cross-Functional Team, other teams in the organization and even the end customer or user, if applicable.

In most cases, a more formal agenda works best for a Cross-Functional Team. However, it is important that the team be involved in setting the agenda to ensure that everyone's information and concerns are included. It is often valuable to have a trained facilitator lead a Cross-Functional Team in order to assure that work and relationships flow smoothly.

The People Dynamics

HOW THE CHANGE STYLES ADAPT

Think of the people you have or plan to have on your team. Consider the four different styles people use to adapt to change (described in Lesson #2). Which of these is the more dominant style for each one of your existing or proposed team members? The following insights will help you anticipate what reactions you might have from each person to participating on a Cross-Functional Team.

Realists will feel pretty comfortable in a Cross-Functional Team, as long as they are asked to provide information and made to feel included in the group. A Realist will not feel comfortable making a decision on the team's behalf without consulting the rest of the team. Some Cross-Functional Teams require this independent decision-making power in order for them to meet timelines.

Collaborators will find it very exciting to meet with members of other teams. Collaborators love the thought of bringing people together. But they may face a challenge if they do not have the skills to actually help others work together to meet a goal. Because Collaborators want to respect each person's point of view, they may have a hard time if there is an emotional conflict.

Goal Seekers may struggle with the interdependency required of a Cross-Functional Team, because their own agendas are typically first priority. This is one of the reasons why a trained facilitator is very helpful with this type of team.

Visionaries often feel very comfortable on a Cross-Functional Team. Visionaries are stimulated by the variety of points of view. They are often very good in the role of liaison between teams, relaying and translating information.

☆ **Tips for Effective Cross-Functional Teams**
Use cross-functional teams when:

☆ Problems between teams/departments need to be worked out together

☆ Teams/departments are interdependent and must work closely to achieve their goals

☆ Star Cross-Functional Teams increase cooperation between teams and can streamline processes or solve problems. Special skills needed for this Star Team℠ are diplomacy and a continual focus on the overall goal.

Self-Directed Teams

Many companies in the 1990's jumped on the Self-Directed Team (SDT) bandwagon for budgetary reasons. They thought they could cut out layers of management and get departments to manage themselves. It seemed like a good idea at the time. However, the factor they overlooked is that SDT's require the highest level of team sophistication. Rather than beginning with a Self-Directed Team, it is something to be strived for after years of successful teaming.

The Process Dynamics

Self-Directed Teams work best when team members:

- Have already been working well together as a team.
- Know how to and feel comfortable with making decisions and coming to consensus.
- Are clear about their goal as a team.
- Have clear roles and agreed-upon responsibilities.
- Have agreed-upon communication guidelines which they live by.

The easiest progression into an SDT is from a Project Team.

Cases

The CALIFORNIA HEALTH & WELFARE AGENCY DATA CENTER had been a traditional data department in 1991 when its executive team decided to join the quality movement. An impetus for this move was the "Compete California!" campaign. This campaign meant that service departments in the state government had to compete equally with private service companies to offer services to other government departments. Yes folks, competition even within the government!

After extensive and continuing training, the staff were formed into teams of different types. After 5 years of functioning together as a team, the procurement team's manager left. Team members decided to continue as a self-directed team (SDT). They divided the manager's tasks and make the decisions together. Coming to consensus is still sometimes a struggle, but teammates say they like the autonomy and have been enjoying their reputation as a successful SDT.

In contrast, another team from the same Data Center lost its manager and became an SDT through attrition. However, this team was less successful, and ultimately went back to being a supervised team. The reasons for this team's demise? It was the unlucky recipient of Team Anointing Process, that is, others decided to label it an SDT. In addition, team members were not given training in how to be an SDT.

WELCH ALLYN, a company which produces medical equipment out of Skaneateles Falls, New York, decided SDT's were the way to go to start their use of teams. One lesson they learned the hard way was the difficulty of transitioning into SDT's from a more traditional type of team, such as a Work Unit Team. Managers had a hard time letting go of their old roles, responsibilities and authority. Transitional facilitation could be valuable in helping managers and their teams progress through changes such as this. A supportive first phase is for management to set the goal and the team to decide on the plan to implement it. After the team learns how to work together, address issues and come to consensus, then everyone will feel more comfortable involving the team in setting the goals. Unfortunately the result of Welch Allyn's excitement about SDT's cost them three of their four teams. Those three teams disbanded with many hard feelings and a general lack of trust about the use of teams.

Meeting Dynamics

Assuming the members of an SDT are already skilled at teaming, the meeting structure should include:

+ Alternating roles (i.e. Leader, Facilitator, Scribe and Timekeeper)
+ Open discussion of topics
+ Consensus based decision-making

The SDT should have the right and organizational support to make decisions that affect their work, such as what new equipment to buy, how to spend their budget, and the hiring and firing of team members. All of these decisions are in consultation with higher level teams. We recommend the use of Ambassadors (see Lesson #5: The New Role of Management) from the Executive Team to keep information flowing. This will prevent an SDT from going too far with its autonomy and keep it in sync with the rest of the company and its goals. This realignment of decision-making is an organizational restructuring of the most fundamental type, and is vital for the success of an SDT.

The People Dynamics

To learn from the lessons (and pain) of the 1990's, advance teams into SDT's only after they have been successful teams of other types, and only after the organizational decision-making structure needed to support them is in place.

How the Styles Adapt

Think of the people you have or plan to have on your team. Consider the four different styles people use to adapt to change (described in Lesson #2). Which of these is the more dominant style for each one of your existing or proposed team members? The following insights will help you anticipate what reactions you might have from each person to participating on a Self-Directed Team.

Realists may find it scary because of the responsibility of decision-making. Realists love to research issues ad infinitum — postponing decision-making. One way to help them come to closure on the research is to set a timeline for completion of the research, while establishing an agreement that this date will be firm.

Collaborators will have a real opportunity to mature their skills of collaboration on an SDT. Because of the necessity for consensus, listening and seeking understanding will be critical development areas for all team members. Collaborators are often the first to step up to this challenge and set the role model.

Goal Seekers will be excited to have this decision-making power. Goal Seekers may have the tendency to go with the first good idea or shoot down others' ideas, but hopefully they have tempered that trait from being on other teams. Use their strength of decision-making to advance the team to reach its goals.

Visionaries will feel pretty comfortable being on an SDT, because of their natural ability to grasp the "big picture." However, Visionaries often have an unrealistic expectation about what can get done in a specific time period and how much it might cost. So it is important to have a balance of the other three change types on the team, or else the SDT may end up over budget and over-obligated.

☆ Tips for Effective Self-Directed Teams

Self-directed teams require high level skills in collaboration, interdependent decision-making and a justified confidence in one's teaming skills. Make sure the team:

☆ Has already been working well together.
☆ Knows how to and feels comfortable with making decisions and coming to consensus.
☆ Is clear about its goal as a team.
☆ Has clear roles and agreed-upon responsibilities.
☆ Has agreed-upon communication guidelines which they live by.

TEAMS SUMMARY

Think about your challenge and goal, then review each type of team to find the right match. Refer back to this Lesson often for detail on the team types you choose.

VIRTUAL TEAM: Members are not in the same location or not on the same shift. They may be spread throughout a building, a city or a country, or they may be in multiple countries.

SPONTANEOUS TEAM: Necessary when time is short; usually project or issue based; short term.

REACTIVE TEAM: Formed to address an issue after it arises.

PROACTIVE TEAM: Typically formed to anticipate problems/challenges that may arise, and then to design and oversee implementation of a new strategy or solution to prevent the problem.

VENTURE TEAM: Minds come together to anticipate future customer, company, or employee needs. Requires effective brainstorming.

PROJECT TEAM: Focuses on a goal that has a specific timeline/deadline. Focus is often on design, development and implementation. Each person has a well defined role, contributing toward the outcome of the project.

WORK UNIT TEAM: Made up of individuals who must rely on working together to produce the results expected for their department. Team member functions are usually similar, for example, programmers in an MIS department.

CROSS-FUNCTIONAL TEAM: Combines people from different teams, departments or disciplines.

SELF-DIRECTED TEAM: Members are highly skilled at "teaming."

In order to create Star TeamsSM, the organization's dynamics and structures must be set to support the people. Evaluation of structures such as training, coaching, facilitation, decision-making and new role definition for everyone must be part of the plan. Creating understanding and appreciation among all team members for each person's change style can help everyone grow into their new roles. The dynamics for exceptional performance are accelerated when the team type and players are carefully chosen and supported by the organization. Now that you have chosen the appropriate type of team, it is time to learn how to redistribute the power, to prepare both management and staff for teams. Read on . . .

NOTES

1. Jessica Lipnack and Jeffrey Stamps, *Virtual Teams* (New York: John Wiley & Sons, 1997), 182.
2. Sonya Prestridge, Manager of Leadership and Teamwork, Center for Creative Leadership, "Virtually Yours: Forming and Developing a Geographically Dispersed Team" (Chicago: presented at Linkage, Inc.'s The Best of Teams '98 Conference, May 7, 1998).
3. Lipnack and Stamps, *Virtual Teams,* 183.
4. *Ibid,* 168.
5. *Ibid,* 168.
6. Ed Oakley and Doug Krug, *Enlightened Leadership: Getting to the Heart of Change* (New York: Simon & Schuster, 1991), 115–116.
7. Colin Hastings, Peter Bixby and Rani Chaudhry-Lawton, *The Superteam Solution* (San Diego: University Associates, 1986), 104.

Lesson #4

Power! Empowerment! Decide Who Gets the Power!

★ Helping Teams Learn to Use Power

★ Three Factors for Redistributing Power

★ Learning the Use of Power

★ Sharing Information Assures Informed Decisions

★ Deciding Who Decides

★ Five Star Decision-Making Process

Stage II:
Planning And Designing A Star Team^SM Culture

Helping Teams Learn to Use Power

In the traditional hierarchical business environment, staff often complained that they were powerless and "if management would just listen to us and give us some authority," then everything would straighten out. In the 1990's, teams were often introduced as a solution to this complaint, and "anointed" with the power and authority to make some decisions. They responded with a variety of reactions, from disbelief and skepticism that they really had the power to "Let's take this power and get all the things we always wanted." The power struggles that ensued caused many a team to self-destruct. What went wrong?

EMPOWERMENT

The use of Star Teams℠ creates a new distribution of power. Deciding when and how much power to give to each team requires strategic thought. If too much power is given too early, team members often fight more because they are afraid to make decisions and risk a mistake. Teams usually need about six months of working together before they are ready for an increase in power and goals.

It is recommended that the first goal assigned to each team be a smaller step with no major financial or product/service risk. However, it needs to be a worthy goal that can have a real impact in making something better. As team members learn to work and make decisions together, then goals and decision-making power can be increased.

Along with goal setting, it is important to clearly define what decisions the team has the authority to make. All too often companies don't take the time to think this process through. The pain often begins to be felt early in the teaming process, when the team begins to ask questions like:

> How much budget do we have to meet our goal?
> How much change can we make in order to reach the goal?
> What kind of power do we have over resources?

In a new team culture, upper management should make decisions on team decision purview. There are two considerations here:

1. What is the process for teams to get authorizations for decisions?
2. What decisions can they make on their own?

Decision areas to consider:

Budget
- How much is allocated for this objective?
- How much can the team spend without asking for approval?
- How much can the team spend on rewards and celebrations?

Equipment
- How much can the team move or change equipment?
- Can the team acquire additional equipment?

Personnel
- Who, besides those on the team, can the team access or pull into the team to assist in some way to meet the objective?
- What level of involvement (time allocations) are the team members allowed to take from the implementation of their job and team goals?

Systems, processes and procedures
- Can the team change existing systems, processes or procedures if they feel it will help them meet the goal?

Interteam involvement
- How much freedom does the team have to involve other teams in helping them meet their goal?

Objective setting
- How much freedom will the team have in setting its own objectives and milestones to meet the goal?

Plan design
- How much freedom will the team have to design or change the implementation plan?

Evaluation
- Who or what factors will judge the effectiveness or successes of the team?

ROUTING DECISIONS UP

When decisions need to be passed up the system, the use of an Ambassador or Sponsor from the Executive Team can help to speed decision-making and increase productivity. This person's role is to attend at least 50% of the team meetings and take team recommendations to the Executive Team (see discussion in Lesson #5, The New Role of Management).

Three Factors for Redistributing Power

When redistributing power through teams, three factors need to be addressed:

1. **What is the goal of giving the team the power?**
2. **Specifically, what are the parameters of the power?**
3. **How much training will the team need in order to learn how to use the power?**

* * * * *

1. What is the goal of giving the team the power?

Power centers around the authority to make decisions. Think about what decisions would be better made by this team. Here are some considerations:

GOAL: MAKE BETTER DECISIONS
The team is closer to the problem, often having information management does not have. Thus the team may have insights into the problem, project or situation that others above them may never think of.

GOAL: CREATE BUY-IN
When team buy-in is important in order to assure productive implementation or functioning, then the team needs to be involved in the decision-making.

GOAL: HANDLE MORE WITH FEWER PEOPLE
When the span of control of managers is too large to handle all daily decisions and problems, then power should be shared with a team. This type of challenge often arises when an organization has just flattened its structure, cutting out many middle management positions.

Once you are clear on the reason to pass decision-making power on to the team, that will help to define what the parameters of power will be.

2. Specifically, what are the parameters of the power?

This is absolutely critical! Lack of a clear definition of power and decision-making authority can cause disaster, and can defeat the very purpose of passing the power to the team.

Case

A Cross-Functional Team in the financial services industry was formed to come up with a better reward system. The team asked management how much money they would have available to implement a new reward system, and what the parameters were. The reply was, "Don't worry about that. Just come up with the most motivating system possible." The team worked hard over several months to develop a multi-level program they were proud of. When they presented it to management, they were told point blank the program would cost too much and they had overstepped their bounds, so none of it would be implemented. The team was crushed and disillusioned. A new wave of management distrust swept the company and no one wanted to be on any teams.

What were management's reasons for passing this decision to the team?

* There had been many complaints about the current system, so they thought they would create more buy-in if the staff designed the plan.
* Morale was low and they thought the participation would create more enthusiasm.
* They had run out of ideas and did not want to be bothered with it any longer.

The last reason was an indicator of a lazy style of management. "Lazy management" can come from being overwhelmed, from bad habits, from arrogance or from a reluctance to make decisions. Whatever the source, this laziness is also the reason why they did not set parameters.

Sample Parameters

Management	Team
Management sets the goal, budget and deadline.	Team designs the plan for how to get there.
Management decides what equipment will be brought in.	Team decides how to arrange it and who will work with what equipment.
Management sets the vision and long range goal.	Team sets and implements all short and mid-range goals and timelines, conferring with management along the way.

Each example in the chart above illustrates a delineation of responsibility between management and the team. The biggest strain on the team happens when too much power or decision-making authority is given them before they are ready for it.

3. How much training will the team need in order to learn how to use the power?

New managers rarely learn to make insightful decisions overnight. So why do we expect a team of staff members to suddenly have this skill? Simultaneously, we throw at teams the challenge of learning how to come to consensus — i.e., getting a *group of people* to come to an agreement on a decision. A tall order, since most managers themselves don't even have this skill.

Learning the Use of Power

What is necessary to prepare people for this change? In addition to helping them understand their own change process (see Lesson #2), management needs to help staff know how to make excellent decisions. It is important to assess the team's resources.

TEAM STRENGTH

Most teams have the advantage of being close to the situation or problem, in contrast to management that is typically more removed. This close perspective can provide a concrete understanding of the cause and possible solutions, thus giving the team an advantage.

TEAM CHALLENGES

However, team members may be lacking in the areas of:

  • The big picture or access to other key information
  • Experience in using a decision-making process
  • Experience in building consensus

To become Star Teams℠ who have learned to use power well, teams need the right information, the right tools, and the right experience.

Sharing Information Assures Informed Decisions

Teams need to be well informed in order to make the best decisions. Traditional managers usually have three concerns about letting go of information:

Managers' Concerns

1. Will I lose power by giving up information?
2. Will they understand it and appreciate its importance?
3. Will they misuse it?

---

1. Will I lose power by giving up information?

Traditional managers are now painfully realizing they simply cannot and do not have all the answers. The sheer quantity of information to digest has become overwhelming. As traditional managers see the necessity to evolve into Star Coaches, they realize that if they can share the information analysis load, the job becomes more manageable.

If traditional managers don't share information, they will fall behind, create mistrust, and reduce their team's problem solving ability. The reason they try to keep information (and this power)? They like to view themselves as white knights, dashing in to save the day. It boils down to ego.

Case

A Senior Vice President of Customer Service was promoted from U.S. to worldwide responsibility. He promptly breezed in to the London office, and upon introducing himself to his staff, said, "Tell me all your problems." He proudly told me of a two page list he left the offices with. He left telling them, "I will fix all of these for you." He felt this was the way to gain acceptance of the people. He acted like he was the only one who could solve these problems, assuming he had information they did not have. He gave them no credit for having any information or insights.

I asked how he was coming along with solving the problems. He replied that he was overwhelmed, with too much to do and had really not had a minute to get to any of them yet. Two months later I called back, only to discover that he had been fired. It was really a shame, because he had been there for many years slowly working his way up the ladder. But his insecurity caused him to think that if he could hold the information close, he would appear more powerful and thus impress more people.

2. Will they understand it and appreciate its importance?

SHARING THE BIG PICTURE

For many executives it is hard to share information about the company's "big picture." This has been the power tool for executives in the past. If the executive team pretends that staff teams don't need the big picture perspective, this indicates the executives don't really support the teams and are setting them up for failure.

Most managers have been pleasantly surprised with the amount of information employees have about the issues close to their jobs. However, when sharing big picture information such as financial status or competitive comparison, remember this is often not only new information, but a new thought for many employees. That's why it is important to offer a short education program about the subject, making sure to translate it into practical terms they can relate to. Offering the company's historical picture opens many employees' eyes and creates great pride in the company. An effective way to communicate this overview is by using a Corporate Life Timeline. This example is the Corporate Life Timeline of the Chicago Mercantile Exchange:

CHICAGO MERCANTILE EXCHANGE HISTORY OF INNOVATION*

1874

The Chicago Produce Exchange is established to provide a systematic market for butter, eggs, poultry and other farm products.

1919

The Butter and Egg Board becomes the Chicago Mercantile Exchange to better reflect its purpose and to accommodate public participation.

1961

A frozen pork belly futures contract begins trading on the CME — the first futures contract based on frozen, stored meats.

1972

The International Monetary Market is created with trading of seven foreign currencies — the first financial futures contracts traded.

1981

The CME introduces Eurodollar futures, the first cash-settled contract, which paves the way for futures on stock indexes.

1992

The GLOBEX electronic trading system begins live trading on June 25.

1994

On February 4, the CME tallies the biggest volume day in its history as a total of nearly 2.2 million futures and options worth more than $2 trillion change hands.

CME Eurodollars become the world's most actively traded contract.

1995

Mexican peso futures and options are launched April 25.

*Reprinted in part with the permission of the Chicago Mercantile Exchange. Taken from the Chicago Mercantile Exchange website, http://www.cme.com/exchange/history.html.

Case

John, an employee at a client company, was a constant complainer and had the attitude that "this is just a job." However, one day he told us that since a recent company-wide meeting where the company's history and mission had been explained, he has totally changed his perspective of his company. He now has more pride about where he works and what the company produces. He then pulled out the one sheet of paper describing the Corporate Life Timeline and current financial status, which he was given during the meeting. He excitedly showed us what it all meant. He now felt he was part of a significantly important company whose products have made major contributions to bettering people's lives and helping the local community. A month later one of his teammates reported that, to his surprise, John had emerged as their team leader. He had new energy and enthusiasm for his job and was taking an outside course on leadership.

3. *Will they misuse it?*
Misuse usually happens because:

- the user doesn't really understand the content or how to use it, or
- the user has a negative agenda

HOW TO HANDLE A LACK OF UNDERSTANDING

Follow this process to ensure that your teams understand the information:

1. Explain the information and its impact on the team, company, customers and community (as appropriate). Illustrate how others have handled this type of situation.
2. Ask questions to check for understanding. Examples:

    - How will you be able to use this information in your job (or to work on this project or goal)?
    - How would you explain this information to someone else?
    - If you had to find this type of information for yourself next time, where might you look or who might you ask to find it?

3. Where appropriate, work with a trainer to create simulation exercises to practice making decisions based on the information (see section below on decision-making).
4. Observe the team during meetings or other times when they would be using the information. Coach when necessary.

HOW TO HANDLE A "NEGATIVE AGENDA"

This is a more complex challenge. Those with a negative agenda are typically people who are complainers, or are filled with anger, habitually shooting down everyone's ideas, or carrying a chip on their shoulder.

Strategies to deal with "negative agenda" people are as individual as each person. Sometimes listening to them, following through on your commitments (to build trust), or giving them some attention can help. Other times it is much deeper and requires consultation with a specialist. Lesson #11 addresses this issue in more depth.

Deciding Who Decides

When teams were first formed in the 1990's, people thought that the whole team should be involved in every decision. Mistake! This approach can unnecessarily bog down decision-making. Use the following factors to choose who should be involved in each decision. Once you are used to considering these factors, you will be able to quickly decide who should decide.

FOUR FACTORS IN DECIDING WHO DECIDES:

(inspired by *Team Training: From Startup to High Performance[1]*)

Time frame: If the time in which to decide is short, then just the Team Leader or a subset of the team may need to make the decision.

Information/Expertise: If only one person has the information, then it may not make sense to consult with others unless the decision directly affects them.

Impact: Team members who will be affected by the decision should probably be in on the process.

Buy-in: The greater the need for team members buy-in, the more important it is that everyone be involved in the decision.

Five Star Decision-Making Process

Americans are usually in such a hurry to make decisions that they often jump immediately to "What should we do?" — i.e., the solution. It seems more efficient to jump to the end. However, a painful lesson learned in the 1990's is that insights critical to preventing toxic decisions can be missed when we fail to consider important factors and think the situation through. The process below outlines important steps to use to make insightful decisions.

The Communication Guidelines described in Lesson #7 and the meeting roles from Lesson #8 both help to set an environment for open and focused discussions. Several approaches may be used to help people come to agreement. One that has proven to be both easy and effective is the Five Star Decision-Making Process. The reason this approach works so well is it creates objectivity (defusing some of the high emotion), fairness, and a focus on goal and requirements.

Five Star Decision-Making Process

1 Definition and Prioritizing

Define the decision to be made, the desired outcome, who should be involved in making the decision, and resources available for the decision.

The "desired outcome" often has many factors or requirements. For example, the equipment must be able to achieve and maintain a specific speed, accuracy, up-time and fit with existing systems. However, the reality is that all requirements cannot always be met. So the team must prioritize its requirements.

PRIORITIZING PROCESS

Have each team member prioritize the requirements. This could be on a scale, such as 1–10, or just into 3 categories (A,B,C), or Requirement (must have) vs. Want (would be nice). Choose which type of scale everyone will use. Then take everyone's prioritized lists and group the highest needs together and the lower needs. This grouping process can easily be done if each requirement was originally put on Post-it notes — they can just be moved around. Another helpful tool is to have the information on computer and simply move it around. In the case of Virtual Teams, this can even be done via e-mail.

★ 2 Gather Solution/Option Information

Brainstorm or research what has worked in the past or for others. Then brainstorm new ideas or options.

★ 3 Qualify Proposed Solutions

In a chart like the one below, list the features of each option, checking whether that item does or does not meet the desired outcome requirement. There may also be additional considerations that are important factors to consider in making the decision. If so, include them under "Additional Factors."

Option	Feature	Meets	Does Not Meet	Additional Factors

★ 4 Choose the Option

Compare all of the information gathered and choose the option that best reaches the desired outcome and priorities, considering your resources available. Keep in mind how the team prioritized the features in Star 1 above. Often, this step is where the most discussion ensues. Be sure to keep it focused on the desired outcome and priorities.

After completing the form, especially focus on the "Meets" and "Additional Factors" area. Compare the "Meets" requirements category to the prioritized list of requirements in Star 1, making sure the finalists address the top priority requirements. In most cases this review should generate your winner.

When there is a tie or lack of agreement, consider these factors:
- Is lack of consensus due to someone not being objective about one alternative because of some emotional investment in it?
- Is more research needed to learn more about each finalist?

5 Build the Action Plan

Based on the option chosen, decide who will do what, by when, and how it will be measured (if appropriate).

Sample Case: A Software Decision

1 *Definition and Prioritizing*

Define the decision to be made, the desired outcome, who should be involved in making the decision, and resources available for the decision.

A Cross-Functional Team has been carefully chosen to decide what software package would be best for several different departments.

The desired outcome:

+ Each department's basic requirements will be met.
+ Access to the information will be increased due to the cross-functional use.
+ More consistency through standardization.

After discussion and scoring, the team arrived at this prioritized list of requirements:

- database capacity for 100,000 names
- fits into budget of $20,000 or less
- handles 20 fields per name
- handles accounts receivable and payable
- easy to use word processing
- customizable

2 *Gather Solution/Option Information*

Brainstorm or research what has worked in the past or for others. Then brainstorm new ideas or options.

The team discussed what had worked in the past and found no possibilities. The Information Technology (IT) team member took on the assignment to scour the market.

Qualify Proposed Solutions
The IT team member brought the results of her research to the next meeting and the team qualified each product. Below is a sample of one of the comparison forms:

Application Software: "Super Duper Pro"

Meets:	Does Not Meet:
• database for 100,000 names	• hard to customize
• with 20 fields per name	• costs $5,000 over budget
• handles accounts receivable and payable	
• has easy to use word processing	

Additional Factors: Our company has worked with this vendor before and found them to have excellent service and reliable products.

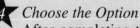 *Choose the Option*
After completing the Qualifying Form, it was clear there were two leading options. Due to the Additional Factor of Super Duper Pro having been a good past vendor, the team decided to approach the vendor to see if they could lower the price, and then if necessary to ask the Executive Team if they could find the additional funds. The vendor agreed to reduce the price by $2000. The Executive Team was able to find the additional $3000. Super Duper Pro was chosen.

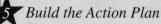 *Build the Action Plan*
The team then met to design the preparation, training and implementation action plan.

IN SUMMARY

The beauty of this Five Star Decision-Making Process is that it provides a structure to guide decision-making. This helps less experienced team members feel more comfortable. It also provides a decision-making trail that can keep the Executive Team informed of the process and status of the decision.

In the Knowledge Age, not only do teams need to learn to make better decisions — so does every business person. These simple steps and factors for consideration can assure more insightful decisions that can make a critical difference in creating exceptional performance.

NOTES

1. Carl Harshman and Steve Phillips, *Team Training: From Startup to High Performance* (New York, NY: McGraw-Hill, Inc., 1996).

Lesson #5

Define the New Role of Management

★ Five New Roles for Managers
★ Managers: Transitioning Through the Three Team Leader Roles
★ The Coach as Performance Consultant

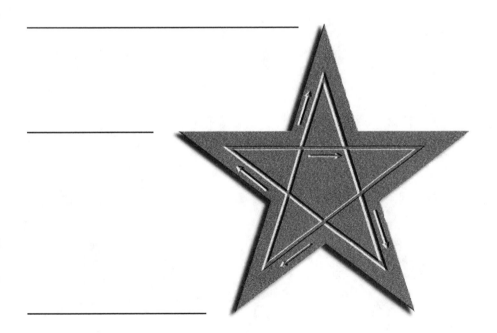

Stage II:
Planning And Designing A Star Team[SM] Culture

> "In the knowledge society, managers must prepare to abandon everything they know."
>
> — Peter Drucker

S o now what does management do? What is the role of management in a team based environment? The simplest answer to that question — and another hard-learned lesson — is "It depends!" It depends on what role is most appropriate for the situation.

Five New Roles for Managers

MANAGER = TEAM LEADER

Some organizations, such as Ameritech, have renamed their managers Team Leaders. The caution, of course, is to make sure you are not just playing name games. To get the most benefit out of the use of teams, the Team Leader must become more democratic and less autocratic, by sharing power with the team. (See Lesson #4 for a discussion of what and how to let go of power.)

MANAGER = AMBASSADOR

The Ambassador can function as a liaison between the executive team and the staff team.

Case

Senior executives at DENNEN STEEL formed a team called the "Leadership & Guidance Team" (LGT) consisting of select members of senior management. Their purpose is to set up a system and environment that will empower the teams, while making sure the teams work toward the company goals. The Ambassador Program was established to help with this goal. Each team was assigned an Ambassador from the LGT. The Ambassador is responsible for attending most of the team meetings, bringing back information or questions to the LGT, and also carrying current information or questions from the LGT to the team. This keeps information flowing both ways.

To increase communication, each Team Leader has a 20-minute audience with the LGT every six weeks. This practice has the additional benefit of increasing credibility and visibility for the work of the teams. This meeting is deemed so important that each member

---

of the LGT is mandated to be there. As mentioned in Lesson #1, Dennen's results are an increase in productivity, greater tonnage per man hour shipped, an increase in pieces shipped, and reduced down time. Productivity and efficiency have gone up so much that they have been able to eliminate one night shift team. Through natural attrition and placing people in other positions, everyone moved into more desirable situations.

MANAGER = COACH

In a team-based environment, one Coach can often handle multiple teams, whereas in the hierarchical structure a Manager could only handle one department. The role of the coach often addresses:

- Helping teams get started
- Helping individuals make the transition
- Attending team meetings
- Assisting with team process
- Playing the role of the Observer in the team meetings
- Coaching individuals to higher levels of performance

MANAGER = HUMAN RESOURCES

The manager can serve more as a Human Resources Center, taking care of paperwork and personnel issues.

Case

In the team-based environment at the CALIFORNIA HEALTH & WELFARE AGENCY DATA CENTER, managers are responsible for performance evaluation, personnel-related type of paperwork, the final say in hiring and conflict resolution. They go one step further, working with teams to form their goals, making sure they are going in the right direction. It took an evolutionary process for these managers to be able to "let go" and trust the teams to take over the rest of their own management. Over a three year timespan, the Data Center committed to two days of training each month. This training covered many topics including change, leadership, values, decision-making, conflict resolution, different ways of thinking, and how to function in a team.

MANAGER = TEAM MEMBER

In some organizations it is felt there is no longer a need for managers — often in a Self-Directed Team environment — and so the manager becomes a member of the team. This may be a valid strategy, but if it is used too early, many people problems arise. Examples:

- Managers feel demoted.
- How is the money issue settled? Do ex-managers keep their higher pay?
- Ex-managers may have a hard time functioning as an equal team member.
- Team members may be confused on how to treat the ex-manager.

We have not yet found an organization where this approach worked well throughout the organization. Success is highly dependent on the attitude and skills of the ex-manager, clarity of new role definition, team acceptance and the evolutionary process used to get to this point. The shorter the process, the less likely the success.

Karen Walkup from the California Health & Welfare Agency Data Center tells other managers that it takes stronger management skills to go into teams. By this she means being flexible enough to change roles, mature enough to set ego aside and skilled enough to support and coach others in their new roles.

Managers: Transitioning Through the Three Team Leader Roles

It is unrealistic to expect a manager who has been functioning in the authoritarian style to overnight be an effective equal member of a Self-Directed Team. Planning for an evolutionary process helps both manager and staff develop into their new roles. One of the quickest ways to lose talented people and create a confused, conflicted, toxic team is to expect the overnight transformation. Following is a sample evolutionary process for both team leader and team members.

TRADITIONAL TEAM LEADERSHIP

Characteristics:

- One formal leader who provides direction.
- Goals are often delivered to the team by the leader as a representative of higher management.
- Team's efforts are guided by the leader and subject to his/her approval.

EMPOWERED TEAM LEADERSHIP

Characteristics:

- Goal is set by the organization, but defined by the team, with guidance from the leader (who functions more like a coach or facilitator).
- Team is allowed to work toward the goal in the way it thinks best.
- Often a mix of consensus and traditional decision-making is used.

SELF-DIRECTED TEAM LEADERSHIP

Characteristics:

- Goal is defined by the team.
- Goal is based on the goals of the organization.
- No official leader; leadership is shared or alternated.
- Consensus is used for decision-making.

As the team leader grows into the role of coach or facilitator, a shift in skills is often required. Here are a few suggestions to use during team meetings:

- Realize that your attitude can set the tone. Make a choice to be alert, attentive, positive and a good listener.
- Be a skillful subtle leader. Do not use your position to push your points.
- Occasionally repeat what someone else has said if you think other members of the group were not listening.
- Watch for defensiveness in others. When it occurs, ask yourself:
   What do you think caused the person to become defensive?
   What can you do to help them open up again?
- Skillfully control the dominant members without alienating them. Humor is often a good tool to use, as long as it is not deprecating.
- Assume everyone's ideas have value.

Another interesting thought is offered by Motorola,[1] which suggests changing the title Team Leader to a term that better supports the role, such as Teambuilder, Conductor, or Architect. Be creative! Put a little thought into the process and what you call this important leadership role.

"The great leader is not the one in the spotlight; he's the one leading the applause."

— Unknown

BECOMING A TRUE COACH

From the manager's point of view, a comfortable aspect of the hierarchical structure is that when employees don't do something "right," the manager gets to TELL them they did it wrong and to do it right from now on. This process seemed easy and fast in the Industrial Age. We believe the reality is that managers were kidding themselves about the real outcome — ignoring what was really happening.

Telling does not work well (especially with today's workforce), because it:

- causes resentment and anger.
- makes the employee feel punished like a child.
- results in a feeling of lack of support.
- does not respect the employee's intelligence or his/her ability to think.
- discourages risk taking or trying new approaches for fear of making a mistake.
- does not motivate the employee to learn from his/her mistake.

The Telling approach causes compounded problems with teams because, in most cases, they are made up of peers. Taking orders from someone of the same level does not sit well with people who are still transitioning from the hierarchical paradigm.

So what can you do? Do the opposite — **Ask!** Use questions to stimulate learning and thinking about the mistake. This also respects the fact that there are different ways to reach the same goal. Next time, the team member may come up with an even better way to do it than what you had in mind.

Making the switch from telling to asking is a major shift. It requires constant self- discipline, especially for those who have been in supervisory or managerial positions for a long time.

What is your emotional reaction when someone asks you, "Why did you do that?"

The English language has created an interesting package of emotional reactions that accompany the term "Why." Whether or not we mean it, we are communicating an accusation, rather than simply seeking information.

What is your emotional reaction when someone asks you, "What was the thought process you used when doing that?"

> In answering these two questions, what is the difference in the type, quality and amount of information you would provide?

Ed Oakley and Doug Krug, in *Enlightened Leadership: Getting to the Heart of Change*, describe the difference in these two types of questions by calling them Effective vs. Ineffective Questions.[2] They offer many suggestions for Effective Questions for performance enhancement, everyday use and empowerment. This excellent book offers many ideas to help build a positive environment for teams.

The usual reaction of defensiveness to Ineffective Questions causes minds to close, and hurts the relationship and trust between both parties. Using Effective Questions helps the manager be more of a coach than a disciplinarian.

COACHING FOR IMPROVED PERFORMANCE

Techniques to improve performance differ in the Star Team℠ setting versus the authoritarian approach. The traditional performance feedback was, "It's my way, or the highway." In the Star Team℠ environment, the Coach works with team members to lead them to understand the impact of the behavior and be part of the solution.

Feedback procedure

The following Feedback Procedure is a process that promotes clarity in understanding and joint buy-in to action steps and responsibilities:

Step 1: Describe the current behavior you are concerned about, with specific example(s).
"Ralph, are you aware that you have come in one hour late three times this week? On Monday, Thursday and today."

Step 2: Describe the impact or result of the behavior.
"When you are late it means everyone else has to do both their job and yours. That causes resentment among your colleagues and puts our response time in jeopardy."

Step 3: Get agreement that there is a problem.
"Do you see how this causes a problem for all of us?"

Step 4: Describe the correct behavior.
"You need to be here on time every day."

Step 5: Ask for suggestions for solutions.
"What suggestions do you have for how you will change things

so you will get here on time every day?"

Step 6: Agree on a solution (and timeline, if appropriate).
"Then, we agree you will get a new alarm clock so you can get to work on time."

Step 7: Express confidence that the person can make the change.
"I have seen you accomplish many more difficult tasks than this, so I'm sure you will be able to get to work on time from now on."

Step 8: Follow up on agreements.
"Let's check back with each other in a week, on Friday at 9:00 a.m., to see how it is going."

Reaching agreement

One of the toughest coaching challenges for managers is reaching agreement that there is a problem which requires action or behavior change. According to organization development consultant Ken Phillips, president of Phillips Associates in Northfield, Illinois and an expert on coaching, "Without agreement from the employee or team member that a problem exists, there is little likelihood that any improvement will occur." Ken has identified four reasons why managers (who are not yet Coaches) have failed in the past to reach employee agreement.[3]

Causes for Failure to Reach Agreement

Managers assume.
Managers often assume the employee:

- understands the issue.
- allocates the same level of importance to the issue as the manager does.
- agrees that there is a problem.

People are motivated to take actions which they see are in their own best interest. They may view their current behavior as most beneficial to themselves. As the Coach, your challenge is to understand what benefits the employee sees with his or her current behavior. Then, share with the employee the benefits to the new behavior and the consequences of the old behavior.

Managers avoid.
Managers may avoid coaching meetings because they feel uncomfortable confronting employees with the need to improve. They may hope that through divine intervention, employees will suddenly discover the

error of their ways. When the manager avoids the issue, what often happens is the employee assumes that it is not — or no longer is — an issue.

Managers generalize.
When discussing a performance problem, managers may speak too generally. They neglect to provide specific examples that help clarify the employee's understanding of what is expected.

"Right string; wrong yo-yo."
Some managers focus on the wrong issue. It may seem easier to get agreement on a couple of incidents, rather than on the overall performance problem. An example is focusing on two late reports vs. the problem of turning in reports late.

The Coach as Performance Consultant

Due to needs for cross training, updating and job changing, the Coach very often must be a Performance Consultant (in other words, a trainer). Training is a skill in which most managers or Coaches are not typically proficient. Nevertheless, the role of the Coach as trainer or Performance Consultant is vital.

KNOW THE ANSWERS

Before beginning training, the Performance Consultant needs to answer the following questions in order to assure an on-target training plan.

- What is the goal of the training? (Be specific, e.g., able to do the task independently in 2 weeks.)
- Do you think the team member really has the ability to perform the new skill?
- Do you think the member really has the desire to perform the new skill? (Know the trainee's motivation level)
- Does the member see the benefits to him/herself, the department, the company and/or the customer?
- Does the member have the appropriate resources (such as supplies, equipment, time)?
- Does the member have a positive incentive for doing the new task or taking on the new responsibility?
- Are there any obstacles or diversions that could get in the way of the learning? If so, what can you do to remove them?

DIFFERENT LEARNING STYLES

People learn better when taught in the medium their mind can best relate to. If information is being transmitted in a way that is difficult for the receiver to learn, the result may be frustration, embarrassment and anger. As we observe people in the act of learning, we find there are three different learning styles: seeing, listening, and doing.

Try this experiment to see it for yourself. The next time you are teaching a person or group, try delivering parts of the content using each approach. Watch the trainees' response. When do they appear to be struggling and when do they quickly "get it"? Most people have at least one learning style that is easier for them than the others.

By knowing how an employee or team member learns best, you can better plan the learning process. This style focus will save time and prevent frustration on everyone's part. Keep in mind that the other two learning styles can also be used for reinforcement and variety.

FLEXING YOUR TEACHING STYLE

After you know the dominant style(s) by which the trainee learns best, then plan to flex your teaching style. Use the following guidelines:

For those who learn best by seeing, watching or reading:

- Provide written resources to read.
- Have them watch while you demonstrate the function.

For those who learn best by listening:

- Verbally explain the process or how to do the function.
- Suggest they audiotape your instructions to listen to again later or find some cassettes to augment their learning process. (Note: Pay attention to confidentiality issues when taping.)
- When appropriate, suggest lectures or programs on the subject or find another expert who can answer the employee's questions.

For those who learn best by doing:

- Get their hands on it and practice.
- Do role play activities.
- Ask them to design and deliver a presentation on the subject.

The following form is an excellent tool to help you prepare for a successful training program.

Performance Training Preparation Template

Goal: After training, the participant will be able to _____

_____

_____

In order for me to prepare for the training, I need to:

- ❑ Know by what style this person learns best.
- ❑ Have the appropriate training media ready (written/visual, audio/spoken or hands-on).
- ❑ Create a quiet, focused environment when possible.
- ❑ Think through how to explain and/or demonstrate the task.
- ❑ Segment the task. Break it down into its parts (give examples).
- ❑ Set description up in a logical sequence. (May be difficult for right-brained trainers.)
- ❑ Create a checklist of the subtasks (if possible).
- ❑ Be prepared to explain the logic or thought process behind doing it a certain way (not just "do it this way").
- ❑ Make sure the key points will be addressed at least three times.
- ❑ Define buzz words and jargon.
- ❑ Be enthusiastic.
- ❑ Prepare the trainee for the training (so he/she will be motivated to learn).
- ❑ Assign preliminary reading, when appropriate.
- ❑ Allocate the time.
- ❑ Discuss the reason, goal and benefits (gain) — don't just mandate it.
- ❑ Have in mind the time goals for progress and completion. (Discuss with trainee and come to an agreement.)

Performance Delivery Keys

DEMONSTRATE

Showing someone how to do the task is one of the best ways to "make it real."

We suggest this two-step process:

1. First time through, demonstrate at the expected work speed. This sets the standard.
2. Then demonstrate at a slower speed, showing the details of each function and what it takes to do it correctly.

When possible use actual on-the-job materials, numbers or props in order to bring more "real-worldness" to the demonstration.

VERIFY UNDERSTANDING

To verify how well your trainee grasps the material:

1. Ask questions to confirm understanding. Be sure to:
    *   Keep questions short and to the point.
    *   Avoid "yes" or "no" questions.
    *   Use Effective Questions that begin with how, what, when or where.

2. Have your trainee:
    *   Repeat the instructions.
    *   Describe how he/she would do it.
    *   Demonstrate doing the task.

PRACTICE, PRACTICE, PRACTICE

Practice helps the trainee gain speed, develop accuracy and handle any obstacles that arise. Research shows memory increases to 90% when the trainee practices the tasks him/herself. Three key ingredients to help assure the success of practice:

1. Trainee practices.
2. Manager observes.
3. Manager provides feedback.

Because trainees are often nervous when practicing a new skill, think about what you can do to help them relax. You can think about what has helped you learn better over the years and also think about their learning style.

Some ideas: Give them breathing room; let them first practice with a co-worker; give them acknowledgment; explain to them the purpose and safety of the practice; let them know it's OK to make mistakes; laugh when mistakes happen in practice. Note: Make sure the practice is taking place in an environment that is safe, both physically and emotionally.

PROVIDE FEEDBACK

Giving feedback during the training process is similar to giving feedback at other times.

Here are some guidelines:

*   Be specific
*   Be immediate

- Make sure it is earned. Avoid feedback that isn't deserved just to make the trainee feel good. Dishonest feedback sets a poor precedent.
- Be positive. Remember that feedback should always be positive, even when telling trainees they have made a mistake. Be sure to:
  — recognize successes
  — correct a mistake in a supportive way, by focusing on the task and not on the person performing it
- Step in, when necessary. There may be times when it is necessary to step in and help before trainees have finished practicing the task. Examples:
  — If they are making a mistake that would cause a major problem or safety issue.
  — If they are performing the procedure incorrectly and it will affect what they do next.

FOLLOW UP

Follow-up is an ongoing process until the trainee reaches a high level of competency in the task. This step involves:

- Time for the trainee to work alone.
- An "open door" policy to answer questions or help solve problems.
- Regular meetings to discuss progress.

NOTES

1. Scott McMurray, "Compensating Individuals for Team Effort," *Insight* (April 1997), pp 14–15.
2. Ed Oakley and Doug Krug, *Enlightened Leadership: Getting to the Heart of Change* (New York: Simon & Schuster, 1991), 138.
3. The causes for failure to reach agreement, and much of the material in this Coaching section is adapted with permission from *Keys To Effective Coaching: Getting Agreement & Handling Excuses* by Kenneth R. Phillips. See www.phillipsassociates.com for more information.

Lesson #6

Maximize Team Recognition and Motivational Programs

★ What to Reward?

★ Motivation: What Does It Take?

★ Important Motivation Strategies

★ Reinforcement and Reminders (R & R's)

Stage II:
Planning And Designing A Star Team℠ Culture

*I*n the 1990's, the question was, "How shall we switch from rewarding the individual to rewarding the *team?*" This was too much of a jump for people and organizations which were still individual focused.

"While most organizations know what to do *with* the teams, many don't know what to do *for* them, according to a recent survey from the Hay Group. More than 240 organizations participated in this third annual survey on teams in corporate America. While 87% reported being more positive about the use of teams, less than half of them (41%) were confident about how and what to pay their team members."[1]

Corporations do not have a good record for rewarding and recognizing individuals, let alone addressing the team issue. In a Towers Perrin nationwide survey of 2,500 U.S. workers conducted in late 1996, it was discovered that fewer workers than the year before "believed their abilities and performance are fairly rewarded and recognized. Only 41% felt that employers considered their interests, down from 50% in 1995."[2]

The need for dual focus on both individual and team is now clear. We suggest two levels of rewards in order to motivate each individual and achieve the team result. To make the reward program effective, it's important to know what each individual likes (e.g., one-on-one recognition) as well as what the team as a whole likes for recognition/rewards (e.g., baseball game or team celebration party). Even in Japan, where group focus is a part of the culture, corporations are bringing in more individual focus in order to achieve a better balance.

In another Towers Perrin study of Canadian managers, it was reported that "only 18% consider program objectives are tied directly to business goals."[3]

Finally, "William M. Mercer Inc. found that the percentage of companies surveyed with team incentive plans increased to 19% last year compared to 16% in 1995. Another 21% of the 2500 companies surveyed said they are considering adding such compensation plans."[4]

What to Reward?

Deciding what you want to reward is vital in order to propel your team to exceptional performance. By answering the following questions, you will be able to target your programs. The more specific you are, the easier it will be to know when you have met your goal.

What behavior do you want more of?
What is your goal?
What are your milestones?
How would you define "exceptional performance"?

These questions can apply at both the macro and micro levels, that is, with overall corporate goals as well as team goals.

Watch What You Ask for — You Might Get it!

When establishing a motivation plan, be careful what you reward. If you reward for immediate bottom line results only, this may cause a shortage of the creativity necessary to benefit the company long-term. If you want to stimulate creativity and risk-taking in order to achieve aggressive results, know that there may be more failures. Famed professional basketball player Michael Jordan, of the Chicago Bulls, missed more shots in one of the 1998 NBA Championship Series games than several of the key Utah Jazz players put together, but he also had a higher score than these same opposing players put together.

Motivation to Mold New Teams

In cases where individuals are on teams for the first time, they are being asked to make a major change in their behavior. Focus rewards on team supporting behavior in order to motivate them to succeed on the team. Focusing on the specific actions you are looking for will help these individuals make the transition into team members. Some examples of actions to be rewarded:

+ a person who usually interrupts others starts listening more
+ someone who summarizes what someone else says before they offer their differing view
+ recognizing someone else's contribution
+ saying thank you to someone in front of others
+ helping to assimilate others' ideas
+ calming a conflict

The rewards for supportive behavior do not need to be grandiose. A personal thank you from the team leader or manager is motivational. Welch Allyn uses personal written cards, a balloon and/or a coupon for free coffee in the cafeteria.

Continuing Teamwork Rewards

After teams learn some of the basic collaborative behavior, decide what additional team behaviors you are looking for. Here are some common ones that come up for maturing teams:

+ When a difference of opinion becomes emotional, switch back to logic and open your mind to options other than your own.

+ Take time before the meeting to organize your research and translate/assimilate it for your teammates.
+ Involve teammates who have been sitting on the sidelines.
+ Support someone who made a mistake and help him/her discover the lesson learned.
+ Handle the "control freak" of the team in a way that he/she can save face while letting go and learning to trust everyone else to have some control.

Motivation: What Does It Take?

When it comes to motivation, it's "different strokes for different folks." After studiously observing people's behaviors in business for 28 years, the author has come to realize that there are seven main categories of motivation for people. Understanding what motivates the individuals on the team will provide insight on how to create the most exceptional team performance. Motivators are divided into extrinsic (motivation stimulated from the outside), intrinsic (internal or self motivation), and intrinsic/extrinsic.

Motivational Factors

EXTRINSIC	INTRINSIC	EXTRINSIC/ INTRINSIC
Crisis, Pressure or Fear	Accomplishment	Control
Recognition	Altruism	
Rewards	Belonging	

Extrinsic Motivational Factors

CRISIS, PRESSURE OR FEAR

Whether they like to admit it, many people are motivated by crisis, pressure or fear. This means they are motivated to do their work only when deadlines are looming, intimidation is used, or they are threatened with the loss of something important to them such as money, prestige, privilege, or job security. Typical symptoms of this type of person:

• They wait until the last minute to do the project because they need the sense of urgency about it to motivate them to get it done.
• They continue to do the behavior even though they have been warned about it many times.

- They tend to prioritize their work according to who shouts the loudest for it.

Sometimes the use of position power gets a "crisis" person motivated. For example, a team leader was frustrated because one of the team members was continually coming in late. He had "tried everything I can think of." Finally he sent the teammate to talk with the Vice President of the area. That is what it took to correct the lateness.

Some people have to go through the entire disciplinary process, until they are just about to be dismissed, before they finally take the issue seriously.

The hierarchical, autocratic style of management has used this motivational approach for centuries. It is based on the philosophy that people don't want to be at work, so they have to be forced and intimidated into doing what management wants done. These negative reinforcers have been used:

- Deadlines
- Intimidation and use of position power
- Loss of money, prestige, privileges, or job security
- Disapproval
- Withholding rewards
- Corrective interview with goals and deadlines
- Disciplinary action
- Suspension and dismissal

This negative approach has been used so extensively that both parties (management and employees) have become accustomed to their roles. It can be extremely uncomfortable to be either delivering or receiving some of these strategies. But there is also a comfort and familiarity to it. It has been done for so many centuries. Breaking out of "needing" to use this motivational approach can be a challenge for all of us.

"You do not lead by hitting people over the head — that's assault, not leadership."

— Dwight D. Eisenhower

TURN PAIN INTO CHOICE

Crisis/pressure/fear motivation is hard on the team leader, the team and the team member. Several actions can be taken to help decrease this behavior for some people. This process is best done between a Coach or Team Leader and the team member.

★ Awareness
Have team members assess themselves on the seven motivational categories. As they become more aware that crisis, pressure or fear is a dominant part of their motivation, they may decide to make a change.

★ Choice
To help them make a different choice, discuss the frustration, anger, upset or "pain" they may feel when working late at night to complete a project or when going through the disciplinary process. Ask if they would like to make a change so they don't have to go through that "pain." They may quickly agree that they want to change. However, making the change can be difficult if this has been a lifetime habit. They may need training in how to do it differently (such as planning a project).

★ Support
After making the choice to change, they will need continual support, which could come in many forms:
• Give recognition when they show the correct behavior, e.g., come to work on time.
• Give reminders, e.g., to start the project.
• Give a nod or knowing look during a meeting when you see them do "that" behavior, if they have been unaware that — or when — they do it.

RECOGNITION

According to Tom Cash of American Express, "Human beings need to be recognized and rewarded for special efforts. You don't even have to give them much. What they want is tangible proof that you really care about the job they do. The reward is really just a symbol of that."[5]

Recognition differs from rewards, in that it focuses more on person to person communications that convey appreciation, such as:

• Verbal recognition ("Thank you!" "I appreciated your support . . .")
• Written recognition (e.g., memo or letter)
• Awards (e.g., a team plaque presented before an audience of other teams)

Recognition can be delivered on a one-to-one basis or in front of others. When choosing whether to recognize someone privately or publicly, please consider their preference. Some people are shy or their cultures do not approve of public recognition. Other people love the public recognition and are greatly motivated by it.

Effective use of recognition is based on Skinner's philosophy of behavior modification: "Catch someone doing something right and give them positive reinforcement for that behavior." Then the person is motivated to give you more of that behavior, rather than the undesirable action.

REWARDS

"To recognize the accomplishment of a team goal that was accomplished, Nancy Lauterbach, owner of Five Star Speakers, Trainers & Consultants in Overland Park, KS, closed down the office for a half day and took the entire staff to the movies and to a restaurant for coffee afterward. At the movie everyone also received money for snacks."[6]

"A manager at The Gap, Inc., headquartered in San Bruno, CA wanted to thank everyone for working madly to meet a big deadline. She gave everyone gift certificates from a spa for a facial or a massage. 'It was a much appreciated treat to help calm down and relax after a tough time,' reports Carol Whittaker, another Gap manager."[7]

Rewards are more tangible or experiential than recognition. Some common rewards:

- Job perks (parking spot, corner office)
- Money or cash equivalents
- Gift certificates
- Time off
- Celebration lunch
- Travel
- Entertainment tickets
- Motivating mementos

To get the motivational result you want, find out what your teams like for rewards. When the author was in sales for Pansophic, an IBM software provider, her "team" met a big goal, the reward was that the entire team got to go a baseball game together. Not a big fan of baseball, she did not relish seeing her colleagues get drunk, shower her with beer and make fools of themselves. This demotivating experience proved to be a lesson in the importance of knowing what your whole team wants and enjoys.

Money or Cash Equivalents

American Express Incentive Services commissioned studies[8] on rewards and recognition. They found that 82% of decision-makers in Fortune 500 companies cited cash as the preferred method of motivation. The reasons stated were its ease of administration, it's what participants want, it's a significant motivator, and it provides flexibility as to how the award can be used.

One challenge with cash rewards is they can easily lose their significance, when the money is just slipped into the billfold or checking account and used to pay bills or other usual expenditures. To literally get more bang for your buck, give money with meaning.

If it is smaller awards to each team member, give it in two dollar bills or silver dollars, so every time they use it they think of the accomplishment. If it is larger amounts, deliver it in Gift Cheques provided by companies like American Express. They are in the form of a certificate that is presented in a prestigious looking envelope. For these larger checks, ask each person to tell everyone else what they bought with the money; or have them take a picture of themselves or family using the purchase. You can post the pictures on a bulletin board to help motivate everyone long past the accomplishment. The beauty of this approach is it allows everyone to get the same reward, but still express their individualism. Gift certificates and merchandise catalogues can be used in a similar way.

The latest thing in cash equivalents is a credit card that has the amount of the award deposited in it. American Express calls theirs the IncentiveFunds Card. Again, it is important to have everyone report on their purchases.

Motivating Mementos

In the last twenty years of the century a new industry really began to blossom — the specialty advertising industry. This rise is directly due to corporations realizing the benefit of using what I call "motivating mementos." When creating a motivational campaign, it is important to have the main message or goal very visible. Printing the main message on objects that the team will see frequently helps remind everyone of the focus.

The most common articles used for this purpose are mugs, posters, key chains, pencils, pens and tee shirts. Creativity in choosing what to put the message on can be guided by these thoughts:

- What will the team see many times during the day?
- What will the team see at key times?
- What would the team see as valuable or useful?

It could be laminated reminder cards, magnets for their file cabinets, or machines or calendars. Some companies have been very creative with their mementos, such as applying the message to toys or food. They became frustrated when they realized the toys were given to the team's children and the candy had a short reminder life. When working with a specialty advertising company, make sure they know about motivation and are as goal-focused as you are. (See list of referrals in the Resources section at the end of this book.)

Intrinsic Motivational Factors

ACCOMPLISHMENT

People who thrive on accomplishment love the challenge. They need goals that are a stretch. They are motivated by the thought that others can't do it or that no one has done it before. Their mottos are typified by these citations:

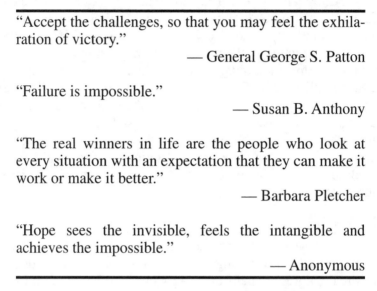

> "Accept the challenges, so that you may feel the exhilaration of victory."
>
> — General George S. Patton

> "Failure is impossible."
>
> — Susan B. Anthony

> "The real winners in life are the people who look at every situation with an expectation that they can make it work or make it better."
>
> — Barbara Pletcher

> "Hope sees the invisible, feels the intangible and achieves the impossible."
>
> — Anonymous

There are varying levels of a sense of accomplishment. Some feel they must surmount extreme challenges, while others appreciate just checking things off the To Do list. We can derive a lot of self satisfaction by meeting our goals, no matter how small or large.

Another motivating aspect for accomplishers is learning. They love to be stimulated by learning new things all the time. Boredom sets in for these people when the job stays the same too long. Self improvement and development are important to them.

> "When an archer misses the mark, he turns and looks for the fault within himself. Failure to hit the bull's-eye is never the fault of the target. To improve your aim — improve yourself."
>
> — Gilbert Arland

Motorola was frustrated because financial rewards did not seem to excite their engineers. Finally, the engineers were asked what would motivate them. The engineers talked excitedly about wanting further training and free time in a lab to work on anything they wanted. Such mental stimulation brings fresh energy and enthusiasm to these engineers.

In business, people who are high in accomplishment motivation have traditionally done well. In teams, they can help propel their team to reach their goal. Be aware that a person who is high in accomplishment may also be a loner. They may need some coaching to help them focus on team accomplishment.

Helping Teams

In order to increase the accomplishment motivation of some teammates, ask them questions like:
"What is the end result of your work?"
"How will it feel when it is done?"
"How can you benefit from having completed this task?"
"Who else will benefit when it is done?"

Help talk them through, and keep them excited and focused on the end result.

"Most people have the desire to look for the exception, instead of the desire to become exceptional."
— Anonymous

ALTRUISM

"There is no higher religion than human service. To work for the common good is the greatest creed."
— Albert Schweitzer

Contributing to a noble cause inspires and motivates many people. The sense of contributing to something that will help others is very rewarding. It contributes to self actualization and is an integral part of interdependence. People who are high in altruism as a motivator often do very well on teams. On the individual level, altruism includes helping others, coaching them, helping them grow, and improving people's lives. On the grander scheme, altruism applies to actions that help the team or organization become stronger or reach the goal.

In a survey conducted by Ernst & Young, LLP, 59% of employees said the best way to motivate them is for managers to show them how their jobs help the company make money. Even in non-profit organizations, many employees are so removed from their clients that they do not realize the great impact their service has. Instead of coming to work to do a task, they could be coming to work to do something as noble as helping to save lives. This shift of focus greatly increases motivation.

Medtronic, a Minneapolis-based company, makes heart valves and pacemakers. Every year at their Christmas party they invite a few of the patients who were recipients of their products. They ask the patients to tell their story of how the pacemaker or heart valve saved their life. There are always teary eyes and full hearts throughout the room as the employees get to realize the value of their jobs.

> "Ultimately, a satisfying life comes from serving other people and making human connections. That is the road to peace of mind, deep satisfaction and greater self-respect."
> — Jim Cathcart, The Acorn Letter

Helping Teams Achieve Altruism

If your group does not score high on altruism, how can you raise the importance of altruism for them? Here are a few suggestions:

- Create a team goal that is important to everyone and could not be achieved if everyone worked alone.
- Teach team members how to coach each other. Often people have never been taught how to guide someone else. Once they know how, use the skill and see others grow and respond, they too can realize the value of altruism.
- Have the team work together on a social service project. It is important here that they actually get to see or work with the people they are helping. Just collecting canned goods does not inspire someone toward altruism, as does working in the food line at a soup kitchen. An individual who is low in altruism can coach children on a sports team or be a Big Brother or Big Sister.

> "It is one of the beautiful compensations of this life that no one can sincerely try to help another without helping himself."
> — Charles Dudley Warner

BELONGING

Abraham Maslow's five steps to self realization place social acceptance as the third building block. Being included in a group creates a sense of security and identity. Sharing experiences with others magnifies the meaning of the experience. The bonding created by working together for a common goal fosters meaning in work and life. At the end of the 20th century, families find themselves spread across the country and the globe. Some of that familial sense of belonging has been lost. Because so many hours of our lives are spent at work, we can get some of the belonging need taken care of by the people we work with. People who rank this category high in their motivation usually enjoy being on a team. A sense of belonging can be further increased by forming teams with a non-work focus for after hours.

"Northwestern Mutual Life Insurance in Milwaukee has dozens of clubs ranging from fishing and running groups to a company chorus. Retirees who continue to participate in such clubs do not have to pay dues."[9]

Extrinsic & Intrinsic Motivation Factors

CONTROL

According to Darrell Mell, Vice President of Telemarketing, Covenant House, "We give employees input into all of the decisions that are made so that they share in the ownership of them. That way nothing is forced on the employees because they're a part of the decision-making process."[10]

Being able to control their work environment is very important to many people. This can range from how they do their job, to the hours they work, to having input into decisions that affect them. Some people don't want to be told how to do a project or their job. You may hear them say, "Just tell me what the goal is or what you want it to look like when it's done, and I'll figure out how to make it happen." They get their thrill out of the mental challenge of figuring out the solution.

One can also see control concerns around the issue of work hours. With a combination of the Millennium Generation's (a.k.a. Generations X & Y) shift in work priorities and the Baby Boomers' exhaustion, many people are wanting to work fewer hours with more flexibility. People who have these goals will often forego a promotion or raise in order to maintain flexibility and control.

In the Knowledge Age, control issues are becoming increasingly important to people. That is one of the reasons for the rise in teams — so employees could have more input. As Gary J. Goberville, Vice President of Human Resources, notes: "If you want a motivated work force taking on the responsibility for good-quality products delivered on time, you have to give them the fullest authority to work out the best way to do it."[11]

Helping Teams Manage Control

What can you do to help? If you have team members or whole teams who are high in "control," try these strategies:

- Empowerment (see Lesson #4): Decide in what areas they could make their own decisions. Check to make sure they have the necessary skill and information to make good decisions in that area. Then give them permission to do it, keeping yourself in the loop for status reports.
- Share information: In the Knowledge Age, information is equated with power. It also relieves fears and helps people move toward action. That is why the "open book policy" has become such a powerful motivator. This is a strategy where management explains the financial status of the company to the employees.

Case

At ARTIST'S FRAME in Chicago, the employees knew they got paid only a fraction of what the customers were charged. The CEO wanted them to understand that the difference between invoice prices and their salaries wasn't all profit. So the employees were given an illustration of company expenses, based on a hypothetical $100 order. Different departments came forward to claim their share of the proceeds. Examples: Human Resources got a share for health insurance and benefits. Marketing got a share for their Yellow Pages advertisement. There was only $5 left as profit.

Result? Improved morale and motivated employees who began to look for ways to save the company money. Now that they understand how lean a company has to run to stay competitive, buyers are ordering in bulk and watching inventory carefully, while clerks are finding ways to handle orders more efficiently.

Enlightened Leadership International, Inc. in Englewood, CO has an open book discussion once each month for the in-house staff led by its president, Richard James. The same information is provided to the rest of the virtual team across the U.S. through a monthly voice mail and mailing regarding finances and company news.

WHERE DO YOU STAND?

The more we are aware of what motivates us, the better we and our team-mates can work toward exceptional performance. Prioritize the motivation options for yourself, thinking about what really motivates you. The more honest you are with yourself, the more insight you'll have into how motivation works. Prioritize the incentives, ranking them 1 through 7, with 1 being most likely and 7 being least likely to motivate you.

	Extrinsic
	Crisis, Pressure, or Fear
	Recognition
	Rewards
	Intrinsic
	Accomplishment
	Altruism
	Belonging
	Extrinsic and Intrinsic
	Control

WHAT MOTIVATES YOUR TEAM?

Think about your team as a whole. Prioritize the options according to what you think generally motivates them as a team.

After your entire team has completed this prioritization, share it with each other. This can be a very eye opening experience. Then discuss this question, "Now that we are aware of what motivates us, what do we want to do more of, or do differently?"

> "Human nature has been sold short . . . (humans have) a higher nature which includes the need for meaningful work, for responsibility, for creativeness, for being fair and just, for doing what is worthwhile and for preferring to do it well."
>
> — Abraham H. Maslow

Important Motivation Strategies

BE FAIR!

> "Imagine a garden with ethics being bright flowers and respect being rich soil. Ethics cannot grow in rock or survive on weak potting mixtures. They need personal attention and cultivation in a place that assigns a higher value to people than to profits . . .
>
> For me, ethics is basically an issue of fairness: fair treatment of people (fair promotions, fair benefits, and fair hearings). For an organization to be fair, it must balance its priorities, giving as much weight to people concerns as it does to economic ones. Overall, to be fair means balancing your natural self-interest with the interests of others. The ethical person knows when to put aside selfish, personal needs and act on the behalf of the welfare of many people."
>
> — Robert H. Rosen, Ph.D., The Healthy Company

Showing favorites was demotivating when we were kids and our sister or brother was "the favorite." It is just as demotivating when we are adults.

CONSISTENCY — EXCEPT . . .

Consistency in treatment builds a sense of fairness and trust. Consistency is a discipline which demands constant self-reminding because it is too easy to say, "Oh, just in this case . . . "

Are there any exceptions? We suggest the only exceptions are for exceptional performance. For example, when the author was in sales for XEROX, she was a top performer nationwide. Her boss asked, "What do you need to help you be even more effective?" She replied, "My own secretary for 10 hours each week." She was given the budget to hire a part-time temporary secretary — as long as she stayed as the #1 rep nationwide. Thus relieved of much paperwork, she was freed up for more selling. She remained in the top position for many months afterward until leaving XEROX to establish the Dynamic Performance Institute.

MARKET THE PLAN

After the motivational plan is designed, market it internally. Have meetings, discuss it in your in-house newsletter, have posters or other motivational mementos. In order to get the full value out of the motivational campaign, keep it visible.

VISIBILITY

Another type of visibility is critical to motivation. Keeping the progress of the team visible not only helps to keep focus, but motivates team members as they walk by and see a chart. It also tells other teams and managers what is going on in the teams.

Both Dennen Steel and Ferno-Washington, an international manufacturer of physical therapy and emergency patient-handling equipment headquartered in Wilmington, Ohio, have a Corporate Score Board (Ferno calls it a "Corporate Dashboard") illustrating the corporate goals and each team's progress toward contributing to the goals. The boards are in a public place and each team is responsible for updating their chart information.

Taking pictures of the team "teaming" adds a fun form of visibility. Catch them during meetings, celebrating, helping each other out, giving rewards, or playing on the volleyball team together. Southwest Airlines puts pictures of their teams celebrating, in airports where their customers can see them. This has helped to endear the Southwest Airlines employees team to customers, creating a loyalty and bond to the company. By viewing the displays, customers can also feel a part of the team.

FREQUENT REWARDS

Dennen Steel changed its reward system from a gain sharing check every quarter to a check every month, in the belief that such immediate feedback is more motivating. Have recognition throughout the year. Then at the end of the year, reward for a variety of categories that would be appropriate for your overall goals.

Case

TRIDENT PRECISION MANUFACTURING of Rochester, NY wanted to try for the Malcolm Baldrige National Quality Award, but realized they could not focus on the quality of the product until they solved another problem. The company had a 41% turnover rate. They focused their solution approach on their people, implementing this three pronged strategy over six years:

1. Give workers more decision-making power on the floor.
2. Spend 4.7% of payroll on training.

3. Give each worker public praise or reward nine times each year.

By focusing on the workers (not the products), Trident reduced defects from 3% to .006%, quadrupled revenue and reduced employee turnover to 5%. They also won the 1996 Malcolm Baldrige National Quality Award for small business. Frequent and visible praise and reward was an integral part of the company's success.

MULTIPLE LEVEL REWARDS

To reward both individual and team work, use a multi-tiered program.

Case

WELCH ALLYN has a three-tiered reward program:
1. Supervisors allocate rewards based on individual performance goals met.
2. Two to three times a year, the company gives teams rewards for their goals met.
3. Individuals can give each other rewards at any time. The peer to peer rewards were mentioned earlier: a balloon, a thank you card and a coupon for a free cup of coffee in the cafeteria. Michael Dahlin, the Quality, Regulatory and Service Manager at Welch Allyn, says this reward program has helped them meet the high standards they set for themselves.

TEAM INVOLVEMENT IN DESIGN

After asking the team what they like in rewards, involve them in the design, development and implementation of the programs. The reward/recognition will have more credibility to the team if they have had a hand in creating it. They may want others to be involved in the delivery of the reward/recognition, such as having the president of the company or other teams join with them in the celebration.

Fabienne Hanks, vice president of sales and marketing for The Meetings Manager, asked team members to create a wish list of rewards — within reason. "It was interesting to see what they really want." Employees asked for time off to spend with family, or to get their houses cleaned and cars washed.[12]

REWARDS ARE NOT ENTITLEMENTS

"A reward is most powerful when it is earned!"
— Janelle Brittain

The paternalistic hierarchical structure gave generic rewards to everyone no matter what their performance. This ranged from giving everyone the same percentage of pay raise to a turkey at Christmas. Soon employees come to expect these rewards as entitlements. They lose their motivational power when they are not earned.

Reward is most powerful when it is linked to performance. That means if there is a category for an award and no team meets it, do not give the award this time. This can provide an opportunity to re-evaluate the goal of the award and what might have been the cause for no team reaching it.

VARIETY IS THE SPICE OF LIFE

After awhile people get bored with the same old reward and it loses its motivating power. A year is the longest time we recommend for one motivational campaign. This does not mean you have to change your goals. For instance, you may still want to have 100% accuracy as your goal. Just change the campaign by offering different rewards and incentives. Beware — a repetitive campaign may begin to feel like an entitlement. For example, if everyone gets a bonus at the end of each quarter when the company is doing well, people begin to rely on it as a part of their pay.

TEAMWORK: A PART OF THE JOB

To raise the focus and priority of participation on a team, each team member's job description should detail what is expected for their involvement in the team. In addition, a section of the annual performance review needs to focus on team participation. The more specific the expectations, the easier it will be to acknowledge progress and give rewards for team performance. Each individual can receive rewards for team involvement and the team can receive a reward for reaching its goals. This is a two-tiered approach.

According to Corporate Director of Compensation David Goodall, Motorola "includes team participation as a significant portion of an employee's job description. Team participation is expected and encouraged, and is rightly viewed as a way to get ahead within the organization."[13]

When you have made the transition to primarily team rewards, use the celebration opportunity to build pride not only within the team, but in the rest of your star organization too.

Case

The CALIFORNIA HEALTH & WELFARE AGENCY DATA CENTER now rewards only for team accomplishment. They have a fund to celebrate team achievements. Even when one team meets a goal, all the teams get to celebrate with them.

DO YOU UNDERSTAND?

Some motivation plans are so complex that employees can't understand them. Even the human resources department, responsible for administering them, may be unsure of what qualifies for a reward. Additionally, some managers or Team Leaders tell everyone what the plan is at the beginning of the year or the project, then never mention it again.

The Motivational Communication Effectiveness Rule is:
Visible, Clear and Simple

Turn your goal into a slogan or even one word that sums it up: such as "100% accuracy."

Reinforcement and Reminders (R & R's)

Reinforcement and reminding are important in order to help people change lifelong behaviors. There are two main categories:

PRINTED R & R

- Posters and reminder cards can summarize tips, techniques, processes or other important information.
- Mugs, matchbooks or any other item staff would see or handle daily can be imprinted with reminder messages. Specialty advertising companies can provide many ideas for appropriate items for your message and budget. (See Resources Section at end of book.)

PERSONAL R & R

- Verbally reminding a teammate at the moment when it applies can help advance a person from awareness to behavioral change.
- Thanking a teammate for the behavior you were looking for helps them focus on the goal and feel success as they progress.

A COMPLETE PLAN

A motivational plan is most effective if it considers the several factors cited above and uses a variety of different motivators in order to appeal to all teammates.

"In a recent study of manufacturing team motivators, more than half of manufacturers say cash works best when combined with non-cash incentives such as recognition programs, training and development, promotions and changes to work content."[14]

Working to keep people motivated is complex because people are complex. But with some communications, participation and planning, it is possible to create a highly motivating Star Team℠ environment.

"Show me an organization where people are working together to do work that they deem important and in a way where they have power to make decisions, and I will show you a place where you don't have to treat people like pets."

— Alfie Kohn, *Punished by Rewards*

NOTES

1. "Companies Still Struggle With Pay for Teams," (March 17, 1997), 3.
2. Gene Koretz, "Job Security is Not Enough," *Business Week* (October 6, 1997).
3. Barry Gros and Marie Szklarz, *CMA, The Management Accounting Magazine*, (June 1997), 10.
4. Scott McMurray, "Compensating Individuals for Team Effort," *Insight* (April 1997), 14–15.
5 Bob Nelson, *1001 Ways to Reward Employees* (New York: Workman Press, 1994), 55. This and other citations from *1001 Ways to Reward Employees* that appear in this chapter are reprinted with permission from the publisher.
6. *Ibid.,* 142.
7. *Ibid.,* 142.
8. From "Motivating Today's Workforce: What Works," a white paper by Patricia Alexander, Vice President, General Manager, American Express Incentive Services.
9. Bob Nelson, *1001 Ways to Reward Employees* (New York: Workman Press, 1994), 142.

10. *Ibid*, 142.
11. *Ibid*,
12. Maria Lenhart, "Winners All," *Meetings and Conventions* (April 1, 1998), 79–83
13. Scott McMurray, "Compensating Individuals for Team Effort," *Insight* (April 1997), 14–15.
14. Bob Nelson, "How to Keep Incentives from Becoming Entitlements," *Manage* (the magazine of the National Management Association), (Feb. 1997), 12.

Lesson #7

Assure Team Communications Amidst Warp Speed and Information Overload

★ Team Communication Guidelines/Agreements

★ The New Prioritizing Rule

"If you want to change an organization, the best lever is to change how it communicates,"says W.R. "Bert" Sutherland, director of SunLabs.[1]

Time is now one of our most precious resources. Today's workers are bombarded with simultaneous demands for their time and attention. The choices they make every minute have a direct impact on whether the next minute will be wasted. An observation of how today's workers have been making decisions is that they are deciding (whether consciously or not) to save time by cutting back on communications — by not using cordialities or tact, not really listening, not thinking the thought through before speaking, and many other bad habits. These all have costly results such as:

- work to be redone
- misunderstandings
- anger, defensiveness and hurt
- mistakes
- lost customers
- missed opportunities

MATH CHALLENGE:

If there are approximately 100,000,000 American workers, and each worker makes one small listening error each day due to being in a hurry and not really focusing, what will it cost business at a cost of just $10 to fix each mistake?

The answer of $1,000,000,000 makes us wake up and realize the impact of poor listening. This riddle only addresses the tip of the iceberg. Most communication mistakes cost much more than $10 to correct. On a team, where relationships are the foundation of communications, it becomes even more costly.

It is a misconception that warp speed communication saves time. Courteous and open communication is one of those things we learned in the past (often the hard way) and are still useful factors for our future success. The following guidelines, when agreed upon and adhered to, create a supportive environment which allows a team to focus on getting the work done — not on dealing with the anger, defensiveness and other negativity that results from warp speed communications.

Team Communication Guidelines/Agreements

Most teams function together more effectively if team members think about how they want to communicate with one another and reach agreement on some guidelines. Following are some suggested guidelines for communication. Discuss these with your team, then check those you decide are vital for you all to observe.

❏ **Really Listen: Don't "Wait to Talk"**
When others are speaking, focus on what they are saying, trying to understand their meaning completely. Don't focus on what you are going to be saying next.

❏ **Be Concise**
For people who tend to be outgoing and talkative, be concise, get to the point and do not monopolize the conversation. Give everyone in the group the chance to shine.

❏ **Speak Up**
If you tend to be quieter or shy, speak up and share your ideas and questions. Others can benefit from your participation.

❏ **Be Open-Minded**
Reserve judgments. Consider all points of view and possibilities.

❏ **Show Respect**
Respect one another while talking or listening.

❏ **Tell the Truth with Tact**
Mom was right. "Honesty is the best policy." However, remember that tact should be used to assure the communication is really heard.

❏ **Think Before Speaking**
Put your brain in gear before taking your mouth out of "park."

❏ **Avoid Derision or Sarcasm**
Making fun of others can hurt communications.

❏ **Seek and Confirm Understanding**
When you are unsure of what someone means, ask for clarification. To confirm that you understand, summarize back to them what you heard.

❏ **Be Open to More Than One Right Answer**
Appreciate the diversity on the team. Each person brings a different skill set and perspective. Accept that there can be more than one right way to solve a problem.

❏ **Disagreement Is O.K., Conflict Is Not**
Disagreement is intellectual, conflict is emotional.

❏ **Additional Guidelines**
What other agreements would be important in order to assure that **your team** maintains open communications?

After your team considers which guidelines to follow, decide how you will enforce them. Here are a few suggestions:

- Have them typed and either posted on the wall or placed on the center of the table in the team meeting room.
- Give permission to everyone to tactfully remind others when they do not follow a guideline.
- Use the Negativity Bombardment Tool (see Lesson #8: "How To Prevent Toxic Team Meeting" — Converting Negativity, Ground Rule #8 for Running Great Star Team℠ Meetings that Get Results).

Case

DENNEN STEEL has become so skilled with communications that they only need to hold 30 minute meetings once a week to address issues and share important information.

HOW MUCH TO COMMUNICATE?

Given the immense deluge of information available, how much information needs to be shared? Too much information can cause confusion and overwhelm. Not enough, reduces decision-making ability, lowers morale and increases anger.

The New Prioritizing Rule

To choose what information to share, ask yourself:
Does this information enable you or others to

- Make a better decision?
- Take a better action?
- Do a better job?
- Feel better about work or the team?

If the answer is yes to any of these variables, it can be just cause to share the information. There are, of course, other considerations like confidentiality or legal restrictions. The main topics teams want to know about relate to their goals and the company's goals.

Case:

FERNO-WASHINGTON'S executive team does monthly "Floor Walks." At least two executives stand in the middle of a department or team area, often with a flipchart. These "Floor Walks" are convened quarterly or as needed to address immediate concerns for their 500 people at their headquarters in Wilmington, OH. The executives present company information on the financial status, new developments, or answers to recent questions submitted to the "Answer Box." This is a two-way conversation with each team so questions are handled as they come up.

The "Answer Box" is an effective communication tool for employees to anonymously ask any business-related question and to receive a timely answer. After the employee's question has been answered, it is posted on the "Answer Board."

They use a form (see next page), which they are glad to share with you.

In Summary

Helping people understand the information is key. This more knowledge based approach is preferable to disseminating information for its own sake.

Poor communications are often the cause for conflicts, defensiveness, trust breakdowns, synergy busters and many of the more fiery, messy team challenges. Poor communication has often been the root cause for team failures. This is a complex skill and issue. By using the Communications Guidelines and the New Prioritizing Rule, you have a good start on assuring effective Team Communications Amidst Warp Speed and Information Overload. Keep in mind that this is only a "good start." Good communication takes constant discipline and continual learning.

Notes

1. Jessica Lipnack & Jeffrey Stamps, *Virtual Teams* (New York: John Wiley & Sons, Inc., 1997), 167.

FOR EMPLOYEE USE

The question is . . .

If you could ask one business-related question of someone in Ferno management, who would it be?

_____

What would the question be?

_____

_____

_____

_____

Response Will Be Posted Within 6 Working Days

FOR HUMAN RESOURCE USE

And the answer is . . .

Submitted To: _____

Date Submitted: _____

Date to Be Returned to Human Resources: _____

Responding Answer:

_____

_____

_____

_____

Lesson #8

Prevent Toxic Team Meetings

★ 14 Ground Rules for Running Great Star Team℠ Meetings

Stage III:
Implementing And Maintaining Star Teams℠

> "It is only when you are face to face that you're able to see eye to eye."
> — Jerome Kurtz

- Ever been frustrated with meetings that are a waste of your time?
- Ever leave a meeting angry because others dominated, sniped or insulted you or others?
- Hate handling tough emotional meetings?

Over eleven million meetings are held in the U.S. every business day according to an estimate from *Business Week.* "Other studies show that managers spend from 30 percent to a whopping 70 percent of their time every day in meetings."[1]

What makes the difference between a team meeting where members leave excited and invigorated with a sense of accomplishment, and one where members leave tired, unmotivated and cynical? The answer is not simple. It involves commitment, discipline and a sense of adventure.

Because time is usually tight and goals can be challenging, it is important to follow these simple ground rules.

14 Ground Rules for Running Great Star Team℠ Meetings That Get Results

1. KNOW THE PURPOSE OF THE MEETING

What's the goal? Why is it being held? Don't hold a meeting out of habit. Time is too precious today. Generally, there are three reasons for meetings:

— to share information
— to solve problems
— to make decisions or plan processes.

Could this information be shared in other ways, such as e-mail, broadcast voice mail, telephone conference call, typed reports?

Does every team member need to come to this meeting? If subgroups are the ones who really need to meet, then don't waste everyone's time.

2. REQUIRE ATTENDANCE

Excuses are too easy to use to "get out of" a meeting. For every meeting missed, the absent team member steps closer to being an "outsider."

Dennen Steel Corp. realized the importance of this ground rule, but had the challenge of a team that crossed two shifts. The team chose the strategy of keeping team meetings to a half hour, positioning it at the last and first fifteen minutes of each shift. This makes it possible for everyone to participate.

3. BE PREPARED

Have an agenda beforehand and distribute it to everyone ahead of time. Even better, design it at the end of each meeting for the next meeting. Part of being prepared for the next meeting is that between meetings, team members must do what they promised to do. One person can be assigned to monitor everyone's progress on their action items. It is advisable to alternate the monitor role in order to prevent antagonism and keep any one person from feeling they always have to play "nudge" or parent to make sure everyone meets their commitment.

Dennen Steel teams do not waste a minute at their weekly team meetings. They discuss, agree on and design any improvement necessary to their process. They also produce their own statistics to measure production and success. They have created an expectation that everyone *will* do their work and be prepared for the meeting.

4. BE TIME DISCIPLINED

Start On Time. Announce in advance that you will start on time. Then do it.

Case

Due to a problem of people being consistently late to meetings, a team decided to require that team members put a dollar in the "Charity Jar" whenever they arrived late. This drew attention to the negative behavior, turned it into a positive result, and helped transform members' discipline and respect for the meeting time.

Allot the Appropriate Amount of Time. Be as realistic as possible when planning the amount of time. Take just a minute before each meeting (or at the end of the previous meeting) to estimate the time needed to address each item, and write it next to each agenda item. Some meetings may require only 15 minutes while others may need 2 hours. Do not assume all meetings will require the same amount of time. Be flexible.

NOTE: Don't be afraid to hold a 15 minute meeting. It's amazing how much can be accomplished in a short period of time when you know what your limitations are.

5. ASSIGN ROLES FOR SMOOTH PROCESS FLOW AND CONTROL

Role clarity is knowing exactly what each member of the team expects or wants every other member to do. Members need to discuss, then choose or identify what role each person will fulfill. Clear roles bring a greater sense of purpose and focus to each member, and serve to facilitate the team toward reaching the goal faster and with less angst.

The key roles to keep a meeting flowing and on target are facilitator, team leader, timekeeper and scribe. Some advisors would suggest that there should be other roles. It is our experience that too many roles causes confusion and a tendency to just forget the roles. In some circumstances, the team may choose to combine facilitator and team leader, but be aware of the power and control issues that may arise.

To build more process skill and respect for each role, rotate them so each team member has a chance to experience each discipline. Many have found it useful to keep the same role for at least four meetings to enable each person to learn their function. Here are suggested functions for each role:

Facilitator

The facilitator is in charge of the meeting process and should:

- Make sure there is an agenda with estimated time allocations for each item.
- Start the meeting on a positive note, with a quick Meeting Opener (see Guideline #5 below), a thought for the day or a bit of laughter.
- Ask at the beginning of the meeting if there are any other items to be added to the agenda and if the estimated time allocations feel appropriate. (Keep in mind these are estimates, but this discussion can help to bring out any subpoints/issues someone may have that they feel require more discussion.)
- Exhibit enough discipline to keep the meeting on the topic, as well as show flexibility and good judgment, when the team really needs to discuss a subject off the agenda.
- Remind members of their agreed-upon communication and meeting rules. (Hint: have the rules posted in the meeting room or have them attached to each meeting agenda.)
- Draw out team members who keep their ideas to themselves.

Team Leader

Separate the roles of Facilitator and Team Leader in order to prevent role confusion and power/control issues. During the meeting, the Team Leader should:

- Listen to others' input before expressing his or her point of view.
- Observe the people part of the process.
- Help the Facilitator enforce communication guidelines.
- Step in to resolve conflict or other tough situations if the Facilitator needs assistance.
- Guide the direction of the meeting toward the goal.
- Bring in information from outside the team when appropriate, such as from other teams or the executive team/branch.

Following the meeting, the Team Leader may:
- Share appropriate information with other teams as a liaison and team representative.
- Take issues, information or questions to administration or the executive team on behalf of the team.

Timekeeper

The timekeeper should:

- Make sure the meeting starts on time.
- Remind members when the estimated time has run out for each item, allowing a decision of whether to continue the discussion, end it or discuss it at another time.
- Give the 10-minute warning before the meeting's designated ending time.
- Lead the celebration when the meeting finishes on time or ahead of schedule!

Scribe

Recording the accomplishments of team meetings in the new millennium is much more streamlined than in the past. A Star Team^{SM} does not waste time with who seconded the motion and all of the points of discussion. Key facts to record:

- The specifics of all decisions made
- What actions will be taken
- Who will do what
- Timelines
- Any measures of effectiveness, if appropriate

The Scribe is also responsible for keeping copies of the minutes for future reference, and for circulating or posting the minutes. Use the updated KISS approach: Keep It Simple & Succinct!

Make sure each team member gets a copy of the meeting minutes by the next day. In some manufacturing sites, simply posting the minutes on the Team Bulletin Board is the best way to disseminate the information. What makes the difference between a team meeting where members leave excited and invigorated with a sense of accomplishment, and one where members leave tired, unmotivated and cynical? The answer is not simple. It involves commitment, discipline and a sense of adventure.

Because time is usually tight and goals can be challenging, it is important to follow these simple ground rules.

• Prevent Misunderstanding

One of the functions of recordkeeping is for everyone to see in writing what they agreed to. The author recalls a telephone meeting during which a virtual team reported on their efforts to try out the new approach for client follow-up. It became clear that as each person went about implementing the new approach, each had different opinions and expectations of who would do what. Some thought the experimental period was 30 days, others said a 60 day period had been agreed on. If notes had been taken and circulated, the need for a second phone meeting to reclarify the program could have been prevented.

• Who Needs to Know?

In addition to the team members, who else needs to know the results of your meeting? Are there other teams whose work is dependent on your decisions and actions? Does the Executive Team need to know? Get copies of meeting minutes to all those who need to know.

• Make It Visible

In order to keep the minutes an active tool, not just stacks of dead trees, copy your minutes on a distinctive paper color. That way everyone will know, for example, that the yellow paper is the Production Team's minutes.

5. Use Meeting Openers

To set a positive and participative tone for the meeting use questions as meeting openers. Enlightened Leadership International, Inc. suggests the use of this type of questioning to open up communications at the beginning of meetings. The questions serve several purposes:

- Answering questions gives everyone a chance to say something at the beginning of the meeting, thus warming up their participation skills.
- Team members get to hear what is on the minds of their colleagues.
- If it's a task focused question, it quickly draws everyone's attention to the subject.
- If it's a fun type of question, it allows team members to lighten up when pressures may be intense.
- Fun questions also help participants get to know more about each other, rather than seeing each other only in terms of their "function," such as accountant. People get to see one another more as whole people.

Rules for effective meeting openers:

- Each person has up to a minute to share their thoughts (this is meant to be just a quick icebreaker).
- The person who came up with the question gets to answer it first (they've had a chance to think about it, and it gives everyone else a second to gather their thoughts).
- If someone wants to pass, they can, but everyone is encouraged to share their thoughts each time.

The questions can relate to the topic of the meeting or the work at hand, as well as information about the rest of their lives. (Of course, one must be careful to not get too personal in the questions.) Here are a few examples:

Task focused:

"What have you accomplished since we last met that you are excited about?"

"What have you learned thus far about what it is like to be on a team?"

"How would you describe what you'd like to accomplish in this meeting?"

More personal and fun focused questions:

"What is exciting that is going on in your life that you would like to share with us?"

"What do you have in common with the person sitting next to you?"

"What is your favorite ride at Disney World, Disneyland or the local amusement park . . . and why do you like it?"

"What is your favorite means of transportation . . . and why do you
 like it?"

"How do you like to eat an Oreo cookie?"

The last set are the type of questions that can be helpful when trust has
broken down within the team and "enemy camps" have started to form.
When people are in an "enemy camps" mentality, such questions help to
get them to laugh and share aspects about the rest of their lives, and also
helps put things in perspective. The finesse of the use of these questions
comes in remembering these two things:

Be a Role Model: If you are introducing the question, make sure you
 are the first person to answer it. That allows you to model the behavior and gives others time to think.

Choose the Right Question: Know your situation and your people.
 Carefully choose the question to accomplish what you want.

Not all meetings need to be started with a Meeting Opener. They are
most helpful during the early stages of a new team, then sporadically
used throughout the year (for long term teams).

6. Remember: Communication is a Two-Way Street

Communications is not just talking; it is listening too. Many believe in the
unspoken myth: "The person who is speaking is the one with the power."
But what happens if no one is listening? Who really has the power?

Synergistic Listening

This is one important difference between teams which are Star Teams[SM]
and those that aren't. The ability to listen to seek understanding (not re-
buttal) creates synergistic listening. That means listening with an open
mind, and suspending judgment until the other person has fully presented his/her view.

Test Yourself

Be honest with yourself in considering whether you have any of the following habits:

When someone else is talking, do you:

❏ fake attention?
❏ interrupt?
❏ think of your own ideas or next response?
❏ tune out dry subjects?
❏ daydream if the speaker is slow?

❏ formulate arguments against the speaker's ideas before fully understanding them?

❏ finish others' sentences?

The more of these you find yourself doing, the less you are really listening to others. Switch your focus to seek to really understand their meaning before formulating your response. It is okay if there is a short pause before you respond. It shows you are carefully considering the points that were made.

Use Your Communication Guidelines

Star Teams^{SM} live by their Communications Guidelines, and by doing so, accomplish more in shorter periods of time with less emotional strife. Self-discipline and mutual support are required to keep the communications positive and focused.

7. ENCOURAGE PARTICIPATION

The People Part

When everyone is involved and participating, they take more ownership and have greater commitment to take action. Humans have a basic need to "belong" to a group. A team fosters and nurtures that need when members really listen to each other, considering each other's point of view and sharing their ideas.

Promoting involvement creates a synergy. That means "producing a whole that is greater than the sum of the parts." Rather than individuals just placing their ideas on the table, and the group moving on from one idea to the next, this means really listening to each other, and considering each point. This respect for the ideas of others not only creates high level synergy, but actually creates new and better ideas. This in essence geometrically increases the results and strengthens the trust and communications between members.

The Process Part

Question: Have you ever been to a meeting where one person dominated the conversation?

Suggestion: Observe who is talking and what percentage of the time they are talking. Notice if anyone is not participating and ask them what their thoughts are on the topic.

Suggestion: At the end of each meeting discuss how the participation went. You may want to ask:

"Did everyone feel that they got to participate?"

"Is there anything else anyone would like to say or contribute about anything we discussed today?"

Star Team^SM Exercise:

Without participation, a team becomes a traditional, authoritarian group. In addition to practicing the "Team Communications Guidelines" and the above suggestions, what else can team members do to promote participation? Discuss your ideas with your team. (Hint: Be creative!)

8. CONVERT NEGATIVITY

Negativity is one of the quickest ways to squash involvement, trust, open communications, and creative problem solving. It can come in the form of personal insults or verbal jabs, negative judgment or authoritative pronouncements. In addition to using the Communication Guidelines mentioned earlier, try these suggestions.

Suggestion: Use the Negativity Bombardment Tool
At the very first meeting give each team member a blank piece of paper. Explain that this is the Negativity Bombardment Tool. Ask everyone to take their piece of paper and crunch it into a ball. Then when they hear anyone lambasting someone else or their idea, just throw the ball of

paper at them. Then, if appropriate, ask the person, "How would you like to say that in a more positive way?" or "We accept your apology."

This is a lighthearted, fun way to help people recognize times when they have switched into their negative, idea squashing 'side.'

Suggestion: Use the rule: "You cannot oppose, unless you propose."
In other words, you've got to have your own idea for a solution, before you can oppose another's idea. This rule can stop those people who spend the whole meeting shooting down the ideas of others, but offer none to replace them. It turns a whiner into a solution focused team member.

9. HAVE DISCIPLINE TO STAY ON TRACK

Catch filibusterers! *Suggestion*: Ask, "Does this discussion get us closer to our goal (in the quickest way possible)?"

Catch red herrings — people who steer the discussion to their favorite issues. *Suggestion*: Bring the discussion back to the agenda.

Catch complainers — people who like to whine. *Suggestion*: When you see this happening, try one of the following:
  • Quickly ask the person what solution he/she had in mind.
  • Offer to make the complaint issue an agenda item at the next meeting.

10. CHECK FOR AGREEMENT

Case

After two days of a strategic planning meeting where much discussion of opposing viewpoints took place, the president of one of our client companies said to the executive team, "Then it is agreed we will follow my plan, right?" He looked quickly around the room, then said, "Fine then, we'll go ahead."

When the leader of the conversation wants to push their point, they may unconsciously choose to ignore any opposition. Additionally, if everyone's commitment is important, everyone must buy into it at some level.

Suggestion: Have open votes, whether vocal, by a show of hands, or in writing for important decisions. Then go around the table and ask each person to describe what the decision means to them or how they will implement it. This helps to assure that everyone understands and agrees on the meaning of the decision.

11. TAKE ACTION

Star Teams℠ follow these guidelines for action:

- Decide what action needs to be taken as a result of the meeting's discussions and decisions.
- Ask who will work on each action item. If no one volunteers for an action item, revisit its importance and the group's commitment to it. It may not be as important to them as they once thought, if they can not raise its priority enough to find time to act on it.
- Decide who will do it. Consider who has the skills, knowledge and time to do it.
- Assign time lines for each action item.
- Assign "buddies," i.e., team members who will "nudge" others to meet their timelines and/or help ensure it gets met. Buddies are most useful for long range goals/activities, people who tend to miss deadlines, or a deadline whose feasibility of being met is questionable. Buddies do not need to be assigned at each meeting, but only when they will be a useful tool.

12. ASSESS YOURSELVES

At the end of the meeting, spend a short time assessing how well the team ran the meeting and participated. Look to Lesson #12: Team Assessment for suggestions.

13. MAKE YOUR PROGRESS VISIBLE

Post your status and results in a public area or at least in the team meeting room. Public display of progress helps with communications among teams, creates accountability and builds excitement. If the poster or status report is displayed in the team meeting room, it can be a helpful tool to keep the focus on progress and the goal.

14. CELEBRATE!

Celebration generates energy and enthusiasm for the tasks ahead. Celebrate every milestone you can think of. Be creative in how you celebrate. Just to get your creativity started, here are a few ideas:

- When tasks are charted out, specially mark or star those that are done.
- Have each person share what the accomplishment meant to them.
- Have each person tell what they learned from the task.
- Feast together on a celebratory lunch or picnic.
- Post an accomplishment announcement on a bulletin board.
- Ring bells or chimes.
- Blow whistles.
- Cheer.
- Sing.
- Say "Thank you!"
- Send cards.

NOTES

1. Charlie Hawkins, *First Aid for Meetings* (Wilsonville, OR: BookPartners, Inc., 1997), 1.

Lesson #9

Trust and Synergy:
The Core of Each Star Team℠

★ Trust is a Must

★ Building Trust Through Social Interaction

Trust is a Must

In the industrial business environment, "Look, you don't have to like me, just do what I tell you" was a common managerial philosophy. Employees knew that if they just did what they were told, they would have a job. Now, in an age of rightsizing, downsizing and disappearing pensions, companies have shown they cannot be trusted to be loyal to their employees. Thus employee loyalty to companies has been shattered. But people have a need to trust each other in order to feel safe and have a sense of belonging. They are starving for this sense of trust.

Through the use of Star Teams℠, people can trust again.

WHAT IS TRUST?

> "Trust is a delicate emotion that takes a long time to build or earn and can be broken in one conversation or action."
>
> — Janelle Brittain

Some vital ingredients that contribute to trust are honesty, humility, reliability, respect, and openness.

HONESTY

Based on surveys of more than 15,000 people, honesty received the highest ranking for important characteristics of admired leaders.[1] In teamwork it is even more important due to the dependency members need to have on each other. Here are some critical questions:

- What does it mean to you to say someone is an honest person?
- Where do you draw the line for absolute truth?
- If someone gives an excuse for not getting their work done, is that being dishonest?
- If someone withholds information because they are afraid of what others might think or how they might react, is that dishonest?
- Are there any times when withholding information is not considered dishonest?
- If you were told that you are not to share certain information with other teammates, but you feel they need to know the information, which is worse? Withholding the information? Or breaking your promise not to tell?

These issues are not clear-cut. They are laced with values and interpretations. Being on a team may bring these issues to the forefront and make people deal with them face to face (rather than behind each other's back). Teams can decide what their definitions are for honesty.

Here is a sample definition for the withholding information issue: In some situations it is acceptable to not share information, such as for personal or personnel confidentiality or security reasons. However, there are many times when information could be shared and the team/employee would find it very helpful and motivating. Ask these two questions when evaluating whether information should be shared:

- Will this information help the team/employee better perform the job?
- Will it help enhance the team/employee's level of buy-in to their job goals?

HUMILITY

The Forum Corporation reports, in a study issued in "Across the Board," that humility helps build trust with colleagues. By admitting doubt or error and acknowledging mistakes, managers were felt to be competent. Co-workers thought, "I can trust you. You won't try to bluff me."

It is important to realize that changing one's position on an issue actually shows strength. People who do so are seen as "big enough" to consider differing points of view and new information, and allow themselves to come to a better decision. This attitude saves face as well as creates a supportive environment for idea creation and sharing.

Question: Think about people you have worked with who struck you as pompous or arrogant. What specifically was it about them that made you not trust them? Where was their focus?

RELIABILITY

When you do what you say you will do, people can trust your word or promise.

Question: How many times will you let someone renege on their promise before you no longer trust them?

Suggestions:

- Let others know immediately if you are unable to carry through on an obligation .
- Take responsibility for your own mistakes. (This means admitting the mistake and taking action to rectify it.)

Another aspect of reliability is pulling your own weight.

Story

Four people were in a boat with a hole in one end. The two people at the low end were madly dipping the water out. The other two at the high end were heard to say, "I'm sure glad the hole is not at our end."

People have a sense of fairness about work contributions. When teammates are judged not to be doing their fair share, a grudge is built and trust deteriorates.

Suggestion: During the periodic team assessment, make sure a question is asked regarding carrying through on responsibilities and a fair share of the workload (See Lesson #12).

OPENNESS

Openness means being equally open to receive and give constructive feedback. Many people have no problem criticizing others. The difference between criticism and constructive feedback is the emotion behind it. Criticism often has a sarcastic tone and wording, with a "holier than thou" attitude. A wedge is hammered between two people when criticism is used. Trust is broken. On the other hand, constructive feedback has a focus on caring to help and understand the other person. It is this caring that builds trust. Some of the toughest times in interpersonal relationships are when we have to tell someone they are doing something "wrong."

Many people need coaching in the skill of receiving constructive feedback. Here are some suggestions for productive receiving:

- Listen to the suggestion fully.
- Resist feeling the need to defend yourself right away.
- Allow yourself to take time to consider their advice.
- Offer your rationale for the action you took. It can help them understand your point of view. But remain open to their point of view too.
- Thank them for their concern and ideas.

RESPECT

At the beginning of the formation of the team, agree on some ground rules to create an environment that supports respect. Here is a sample agreement:

To show respect, each team member will:

- Listen to the ideas expressed by others.
- Refrain from interrupting when others are speaking.
- Give the "experts" on the team a greater weight in any discussion which involves their expertise. (This does not mean others cannot offer differing opinions.)

Teams often decide on their own respect rules as problems arise. A Star TeamSM sets them up at the time the team is established.

Building Trust Through Social Interaction

Build trust among team members by creating opportunities for team members to have social interaction. One of the key elements in trust is knowing each other as whole people, not just as a "function." Social interaction is one approach to bridging to trust. Social interaction is especially important for Virtual Teams because members do not see one another as much as those on other teams.

INCREASING TEAM SYNERGY

"The world basically and fundamentally is constituted on the basis of harmony. Everything works in cooperation with something else."

— Preston Bradley

Internal team support is vital to assuring continuing synergy. Support (or the lack of it) is shown between team members in every interaction they have. One-to-one interactions are the building blocks of team synergy — but only when everyone is working together well.

Here are the most common Synergy Busters:

- An inconsiderate communication
- Not pitching in when another team member really needs help
- A win/lose conflict

PERSONAL SYNERGY BUILDERS & BUSTERS

A Star Team[SM] is created when synergy is positive among all team members. When there are negative interactions, they need to be recognized and resolved. We advocate that each team member conduct a periodic personal assessment of how he or she has worked with the other members. The Synergy Star may be used for this analysis. Here is an example:

Ken
Worked well with Ken
to design plan.

ME

Sue
Lambasted her idea.
(I will apologize and
be more open-minded
in the future.)

Mark
Argued about job responsibilities without
resolution. (I will meet
with Mark and search
for a win/win solution.)

Laurie
Ignored her suggestions.
(I will apologize and listen
more carefully in the future.)

John
Worked well with John
on accounting problem.

167

It is important to write what action will be taken to correct any synergy busting behavior. Team members may want to share what they wrote in order to expedite communications and synergy repair work. This periodic assessment helps to clear the air and prevent the proverbial molehills from turning into mountains.

Some people are afraid to trust others because it feels like they are giving up control.

Actually, trusting others actually frees everyone up, giving everyone more control. By not having to deal with paranoia and micromanaging, we are able to focus on our goal and to think more strategically, while enjoying working with each other.

"What sets apart high performance teams is the degree of commitment, particularly how deeply committed the team members are to one another."[2]

— The Wisdom of Teams

NOTES

1. James M. Kouzes and Barry Z. Posner, *Credibility: How Leaders Gain and Lose It, Why People Demand It* (San Francisco: Jossey-Bass Inc.)
2. Jon R. Katzenbach and Douglas K. Smith, *The Wisdom of Teams* (New York: HarperCollins Publishers, 1994), 65.

Lesson #10

Transform Conflict into a Difference of Opinion

★ Understanding The Situation

★ The DOO Approach

★ When Things Have Built Up . . .

★ The Benefits of a Difference of Opinion

★ The Five Conflict Management Styles

★ Resolution Techniques

Stage III:
Implementing And Maintaining Star Teams^{SM}

ICEBERG THEORY OF TEAMS

Team Riddle: What percentage of an iceberg is generally sticking up?
Answer: 10%
Is it the tip that causes the shipwreck?

Question: What do conflicts seem to be about?
Answer: Tasks

If we look at the whole picture, tasks are usually only 10% of the conflict. Relationships are 90%. Your team will never be shipwrecked over a task — only over a relationship.

* * * * *

"Don't you know better than that? I told you to do it this way."

"Yes, but usually . . . "

"I don't care what usual procedures are, just do it my way and do it now!"

"But what about . . . "

"I don't care what else you are doing or what anyone else will say about it — just do it!"

"Yes sir."

* * * * *

"The right way to do this is to bring in a new computer."
"No way, we can't afford it. We can get along just fine with paper and pencil."
"You've got to be kidding me. What a waste of time. The real reason is you are just afraid of computers and you don't want to learn. You are stuck in the Dark Ages."
"Computers are not the answer to everything. People still matter. I give up on you. If you bring in a computer, I'll refuse to use it."
The inability to handle "conflict" is a common reason for a team to fall apart. In this transition period, our challenge is that we are still applying the conflict styles of authoritarian times to our new ways of relating. WE NEED TO LEARN NEW SKILLS!

Understanding The Situation

The authoritarian style (derived from the military) supported two styles or roles in a conflict: the authoritarian and the doer or obedient one. The outcome had to be a win/lose. Our challenge today is that the employees are better educated and have a stronger sense of their own self-worth and greater confidence about their decision-making abilities. Many "refuse to take it anymore." Employers see their valued employees walking out the door simply because their managers don't know any other style than the authoritarian.

As the workforce has changed, many authoritarian style managers have been slow to change or adapt. This has caused an explosion of work related lawsuits.

It's time to make the shift from the intense battle focused approach to a more relaxed perspective we call the DOO — a Difference Of Opinion.

The DOO Approach

Viewing the discussion from the DOO approach requires a shift in perspective — seeing it as a Difference Of Opinion, not a conflict.

Conflict means "I am right and you are wrong." In conflict, there is typically very little listening to the other person's views, and high emotional attachment to one's own ideas. The goal of conflict is to win — no matter what.

Common phrases:
"The right way is . . . "
"You are wrong."

Aha's About Conflict
- People in conflict typically believe they know the cause of the conflict, BUT their diagnosis is almost always in error.
- Conflicts perceived to be rooted in action and content are, in reality, are often caused by communication failures, particularly in listening.
- Deliberate attempts to harm another person are extremely rare.
- The need to be right — a basic drive in most of us — is a primary contributor to many conflicts.
- By the time conflict reaches a level where people are willing to deal with it, the real conflict is actually an

accumulation of half-remembered and relatively minor issues.
- Most conflicts involve a dance — a series of moves and counter-moves by each party — with each person wanting to lead.

Recognizing a situation as a difference of opinion switches each person into a more logical discussion mode and more open listening mode. DOO is not accusatory, so each person takes accountability for the fact that what they are expressing is their point of view. The goal of a DOO discussion is to come to resolution.

Common phrases:

"My opinion is . . . "

"I have observed that . . . "

"I want to understand where you are coming from . . . "

"In other words, you are saying that . . . " (summarize the other person's point, without derision or sarcasm.)

SUGGESTIONS

+ Focus on how this sharing of different points of view can help reach our goal. If discussion is irrelevant to the goal, decide to set it aside, handle it afterward or make another appropriate decision to bring the discussion back to the point.
+ Appeal to a higher power or greater good, such as for the sake of the team, for reaching the goal, or for helping the customer.
+ Let the other party save face, unless you want to start a "revenge account" that earns compound interest.

When Things Have Built Up . . .

When two people are not getting along, their focus may need some help. This is a time when a facilitator can guide the two back toward resolution. In this situation, the goal is to help relieve the relationship pressure so the two can get back to working together. The facilitator can guide both individuals through this series of four reconciliation questions:

Reconciliation: We Can Do It!

1. What do you respect about this person?

Have each person say something they respect about the other person. Usually they will test the waters out by providing a superficial response, like, "Well, he dresses nice." The facilitator should keep asking for more things they respect about each other until they provide more substantial, work relationship responses, such as, "She really seems to care about doing a good job."

2. What do you have in common with this person?
Again, if they come up with superficial responses, keep asking "What else do you have in common?" In this case even providing personal responses can be helpful, such as "We both have children." Getting them to talk about their kids can help ease the tension. The point of this questioning is to dissipate the "enemy camp" feeling between the two people and help them realize the other person isn't all bad.

3. What do you like about this person?
By this time they should be ready to share something they actually like about each other. You will usually start to see a smile on their faces as they answer this question.

4. What is working in your work relationship?
By listing what is working, they can learn from their successes. The items that are bothering one another and need to be discussed are now put in the context of "This is a person I can work with. We just need to work through this one issue." This process allows each person to save face, builds their self-esteem and opens them up to listening to the other person.

The Benefits of a Difference of Opinion

Given that we have new and more complex problems than ever before, considering multiple possibilities can help us come up with better solutions.

* **Enjoy the Difference**
  Appreciate the diversity on the team. Each person brings a unique set of skills and perspectives. A difference of opinion can cause new insights to occur on all sides.

* **More Than One Way**
  Accept that there can be more than one right way to solve a problem.

* **Take the Time**
  Know that it will take more time to look for more than one answer. Often we are in such a hurry that we jump on the first good idea that comes up. Confirm that the first idea was a very good one,

then ask some of the following questions to stimulate additional thoughts:
- Would anyone like to build on the first idea?
- Does anyone else have another idea?
- What have others done in other departments, companies or industries when faced with a similar situation?

As ideas are shared, individuals may have emotional attachments to their ideas. This can often cause a conflict. One job of the Team Leader and Facilitator is to keep reminding everyone that we value all ideas and each may have a role in the development of the final plan.

DEFENSIVE CHARACTERISTICS[1]
What often tends to cause defensiveness is a sense that someone:
- Is evaluating us or watching for us to make a mistake.
- Is trying to control or manipulate us.
- Doesn't care about us.
- Considers themselves superior, or to know it all.

SUPPORTIVE CHARACTERISTICS
We tend to communicate openly with people who seem to be:
- + Cooperating in solving a problem.
- + Acting with sincerity.
- + Concerned with our welfare.
- + Considering themselves equal to us.
- + Open to the ideas of others.

The Five Conflict Management Styles

Because we need to transition from the bipolar conflict style of the authoritarian times, knowing when and how to use the following five conflict management styles can help us break out of our rut. Each of these styles is appropriate to use at different times. As you read about each style ask yourself:

- Which style do I tend to use the most?
- Which style do I need to use more?
- Which style does my nemesis use?

Each style is helpful in certain situations, while at other times it can be very detrimental.

THE ACCOMMODATING STYLE

"Yes Sir/Ma'am."

In the authoritarian days, most employees were expected to be compliant. They were supposed to follow orders/instructions without a whimper, comment or suggestion. Believe it or not, there is still a place for this style. When you feel having a conflict or expressing your view would damage the relationship, then the accommodating style is often worth it. Additionally, if you really don't care about the issue, be accommodating to the other person's view.

An important tip about the use of the accommodating style: if you decide to accommodate, let go of any ownership for other views you may have. Any anger you retain about not getting your own way will hurt you worse than it will the other person. As long as you make a conscious decision to accommodate, make a conscious decision to enjoy doing it the other person's way. Also keep in mind there will be other times when you will get your way on things that are more important to you.

Customer Service

The accommodating style is very appropriate in a service situation. If you follow the axiom "The customer is always right," then accommodating is important. The challenge comes when employees who are constantly accommodating feel they are losing their own identity. Here are some ideas to address this situation:

- Allow staff to have input into decisions about things in their work area.
- Ask staff to keep track of customer suggestions and concerns, and use this documentation as resource information to improve ser-

vice. (This practice allows staff to see complaints as important information and not to take them personally if it's not appropriate. It also lets them know they have some power in the situation —that they are not just a doormat for management's mistakes.)

THE AVOIDING STYLE

"It's not really a problem."
"It'll go away in awhile if I just don't pay any attention to it."

Because the majority of the workforce has not been trained in how to handle a difference of opinion (and probably have very negative experiences because of that), they tend to avoid conflict. Unfortunately, continually avoiding an issue that really needs attention usually turns the disagreement into an explosion when the avoider "can't take it anymore." The explosion can happen either internally or externally.

Dealing with Anger

Often people's biggest challenge is learning how to discharge or address anger in a way that is both acceptable in society and healthy for the self.

Suppressing vs. Repressing

When you are "suppressing" your anger, you are *consciously* choosing to hold your anger back.

When you are "repressing" your anger, you are *unconsciously* choosing to hold back your anger. Research shows continually suppressed and repressed anger seems to be an apparent cause in various kinds of cancer, rheumatoid arthritis, ulcerative colitis, depression and high blood pressure.

Expressing

Expressing your anger can physically cause elevated blood pressure, increased heart rate, increased blood sugar, as well as constricted blood vessel to the digestive tract. Type A men are more prone to heart disease. One of the determining factors is that they express their anger outward and become angry more than once per week. Research shows that women who were either very seldom angry or highly volatile were more likely to have malignant tumors.

A Solution: Reflecting

Cool reflection occurs when you acknowledge your anger, then choose to:

1. cool down first
2. discuss the conflict reasonably with the goal of resolution.

Physical reactions to this approach include lower blood pressure and a much healthier body overall.

Avoidance is best used when:

- Conflict is truly small and will not mount into a larger issue.
- It is an incidental behavior you choose not to promote by giving it attention, because you think it is a one time "test".
- You make a conscious choice to avoid the issue (not just "let it happen").

When choosing avoidance, do be aware that if the issue or behavior arises again, a different style may be required.

THE DOMINATING STYLE

"Do it my way — and now!"

In the authoritarian management style, anger was the only acceptable emotion. The John Wayne approach to conflict was the respected "macho" way. Managers were trained in this style. Our society gave them permission to, in essence, walk around with their "six guns" ready to fire

— just looking for a reason to yell at someone.

This dominating style is not working today and is part of the reason for the evolution into teams. However there are a few times when this style may be appropriate. If the situation involves an emergency, such as during a fire alarm, then barking out orders as to which door to take is appropriate. Some would say that the dominating style is appropriate when you must win at any cost. This author's concern is — the cost. The price is paid in trust and a willingness to work together. This can break a team apart.

THE COMPROMISING STYLE

"I think this is the right way to do this procedure, but since we need to work together, let's talk about it."

The compromising style is aggressive, but co-operative. Compromisers see that they must give up some in order to get a part of what they want. However, there may still be a chip on their shoulder because they had to give up something.

This style may also be appropriate if there is a stalemate and bringing in a third party to help mediate becomes necessary. The Team Leader or Facilitator could serve as the mediator.

The compromising style is best when no one solution can

Compromise = Give some to get some   satisfy everyone.

THE COLLABORATIVE STYLE

"I'm used to doing it this way, but I'm interested in learning more about your way."

The collaborating style shows respect for everyone's point of view. Collaborators do not diminish their own point of view, yet they are open to the views of others as well. Their focus is more on fixing the problem than on fixing  blame. They view the situation as a difference of opinion and as resolvable. They take an enlightened approach of looking for what each person *really* wants or needs. They follow the DOO approach.

The collaborative style works best when the other parties are using the same style. However, it can also be used successfully to help bring out the avoiding and accommodating people so they will share their ideas. When used with the dominating style, it can have the effect of either calming down the emotions of the dominator, or providing an opportunity for the dominator to walk all over the collaborator. When used with the compromiser, it can help reduce their grudge factor.

> "A hurricane: many individual raindrops collaborating."
> — Unknown

This summary chart can be helpful for reference after you understand each style.

The Five Conflict Management Styles

The Accommodating Style
"Yes Sir/Ma'am"
Characteristics:
    Agreeable
    Non-assertive
    Cooperates even at expense of personal goals
    Blames self
    Suppresses anger
Best used when:
Conflict is not worth the risk of damaging the relationship

The Avoiding Style
"It's not really a problem."
Characteristics:
    Non-confrontational
    Denies issues are a problem
    Expects resolution to occur spontaneously
    Patient
    Chooses not to act or decide
    Represses anger
Best used when:
    Conflict is very small
    The issue is not important to you
    The situation is not worth the risk or effort to fight

The Dominating Style
"Do it my way — and now!"

Characteristics:
Confrontational
Aggressive
Demanding
Blames others
Impatient
Fully expresses anger
Best used in:
An emergency

The Compromising Style
"I think this is the right way to do this procedure, but since we need to work together, let's talk about it."
Characteristics:
Aggressive but cooperative
Willing to give some in order to get some
Seeks others to help resolve conflict
Best used when:
No one solution is perfect
There is more than one good way to address issue
You must give to get what you want

The Collaborative Style
"I'm used to doing it this way, but I'm interested in learning more about your way."
Characteristics:
Assertive and cooperative
Shows mutual respect
Considers both sides
Takes action toward resolution quickly
Views conflict as OK
Interested in fixing the problem, not the blame
Best used when:
All parties openly discuss the issues
A mutually beneficial solution can be found without anyone making a major concession

Resolution Techniques

Different conflict situations require various approaches for resolving them. Following is a treasure chest of gems to pull out when you need them. Put a check mark before those you want to remind yourself to use more frequently or for specific types of situations.

❐ **Innocent until proven guilty**
Give the other person the benefit of the doubt until all facts are collected.

❐ **Find out the motivation**
Gaining an understanding of someone's thoughts or rationale is proven to be among the fastest ways to resolve a conflict. This approach of "walking in the other person's shoes" can shed new light on the discussion.

❐ **Provide key information**
Be sure to share information that is important to the situation.

❐ **Attack the problem, not the person**
Be tough on the problem and soft on the person.
Tact is an important tool here.

❐ **Show commonalities**
Find something you have in common. *Example*: We both want to help the customer."

❐ **Never respond to a hostile remark with a hostile remark**
This dynamic only escalates the argument.

❐ **Rarely issue an ultimatum**
It backs both of you into corners.

❐ **Take responsibility**
Use "I" instead of "you" statements. *Examples*:
"You're wrong." *Bad*
"I feel that I am right." *Good*

❐ **Listen and Summarize**
Keep an open mind while listening. Then prove you listened by Summarizing. Repeat back to the person what you heard them say — to their satisfaction. Remember to summarize without sarcasm.

❐ **Call a Ground Rule**
When other team members see that one member is not listening to another, they can "call" a ground rule and require the poor listener to summarize back the other's message to their satisfaction. Then they can make their point. The offender may need to summarize several times during the conversation, whenever it becomes evident that they are not listening. This technique helps to build good listening habits, especially when emotions are high.

❐ **Support each other**

When you know someone on staff is hurting, acknowledge it. People in emotional pain need support. They need you to notice and say, "I'm sorry you're hurt."

IN SUMMARY

Learning how to turn conflict into an open exchange of ideas is an integral part of the Star Team℠. Realistically, it may take considerable time — especially for some team members — to make the transition. The key is to set agreements for openness and maintain it as a standard expectation of the team. If all team members help remind, support, and understand each other, the process will progress faster and with less pain.

NOTES

1. Defensive and supportive characteristics adapted from J.R. Gibb, "Defensive Communication," *Journal of Communication*, vol. 11, No.3 (September 1961), 141–148.

Lesson #11

Deal with the "Tuff Stuff"

★ Understanding The "Problem People"

★ Handling Emotional Communications

★ Low Morale Due to Changes

★ Common Cause: Low Self-Esteem

★ How To Remove a Team Member

Stage III:
Implementing And Maintaining Star Teams^{SM}

*I*n conversations with organizations that implemented teams in the 1990's, we observed that their greatest pain came when they described some of their people problems. In most cases they did not know how to deal with these types of problems, so either they put their head in the sand — ignoring the problem, or they fired the person. The result was either the problem got worse or they lost a person who had years of valuable experience and knowledge. Dealing with the psychological aspects of people is something new for organizations. These issues used to be shuffled off the Human Resources Department. Now Team Leaders, Facilitators and Team Members need to learn how to work with the psychological aspects of one another. We call this the "Tuff Stuff."

Understanding The "Problem People"

The managers at Quill Corporation, an office supply company in Illinois, had an interesting insight as they were implementing teams. They noticed that each team had at least one HMI ("High Maintenance Individual"). During the transition, managers met at 7:00 AM each day to discuss purpose, roles, rules and problems. They discovered they were spending the majority of their time talking about the HMI's.

By understanding the people on our team who cause us the most angst, we can learn how to help them become exceptional performers.

WHAT MOTIVATES THEM?

By analyzing what motivates our "problem person," we may learn how to tap into their positive contribution. After this analysis, many discover that their team setup does not emphasize what really revs this person's engines. To do this analysis, turn back to "Lesson #6: Maximize Team Recognition and Motivational Programs." As you look at the seven categories, prioritize the options you think motivate this person or ask them to rank the categories. This is a good time to talk with the problem person about what motivates them.

Handling Emotional Communications

Dealing with an emotionally charged issue is a true test of one's ability to work well with others. Following is a suggested process to assure that two-way communications are open and high emotion is prevented.

1. LISTEN ACTIVELY

Summarize back to the other person what you heard them say. Make sure there is no derision or sarcasm in your response. You can even say, "I can hear that this is very important to you." This lets them know that you are not only listening to their words, but "listening between the lines."

2. SEEK UNDERSTANDING: ASK CLARIFYING QUESTIONS

Rather than reacting to what the person says, focus on making sure you understand it thoroughly. Ask questions such as:

> "I understand that SVGA screens are important to you. Can you tell me more about how they will help you in your job?"

> "I understand that you prefer to use paper and pencil rather than a computer. What are your thoughts on how you can increase your productivity by the 25% we need?"

The person may have information and ideas that can clear up the situation. Sometimes the questions help the person think through the situation. Effective Questions help people discover their own answers. (For more information on constructing Effective Questions, see the coaching section of Lesson #5: Define The New Role of Management.)

3. TACTFULLY MAKE YOUR POINT

Explain your point of view or idea with sincerity (not with an attitude of "My idea is better than your stupid idea.") Use a confident but friendly tone.

4. BUILD A SOLUTION FROM EVERYONE'S IDEAS/NEEDS

Look for and mention areas where both of your ideas are similar or build on each other. Usually a vocal "problem person" simply wants to be heard and to have their ideas considered.

In most cases, once the "problem person" sees that you are interested in listening and working together, they will calm down.

Low Morale Due to Changes

Change in the third millennium is a constant. Even though we are getting more practice at handling it, we can still experience insecurity, upset, confusion and fear when trying to deal with it. The "People" section of Lesson #2 offers many suggestions to help with these transitions.

If your challenge needs additional help, consider these solutions.

SOLUTION 1:
PROVIDE INFORMATION AS EARLY AS POSSIBLE.

The 1980's and 1990's have provided new insight about low morale. As we observe companies going through downsizing, rightsizing, reengineering, mergers or layoffs, we consistently see morale lowest during times when employees do not know the specifics about their future. Once they know whether they are staying, leaving or changing job functions, they can plan and take action. Often management has withheld information until the last minute, then expected people to accept it and move on. This approach is sure to cause angst and strife for everyone involved. Share information as soon as you have it.

SOLUTION 2: BE SUPPORTIVE AND UNDERSTANDING

Recognize that this is a time of special strain for people. Make sure your door is truly "open," offering a place to come and talk.

SOLUTION 3: COACH EMPLOYEES INTO ACTION

Once an announcement is made regarding the changes, allocate time to meet with each person to coach them through their action steps. Once people start to take action, they usually feel more in control of the situation.

SOLUTION 4: LOOK TO THEIR STRENGTHS

Help employees focus on their strengths and what is not changing. This will direct their attention and actions to areas where they can excel. By focusing on what is staying stable, you are helping employees feel more calm and centered.

SOLUTION 5: SEEK OTHER RESOURCES

There may be times when employees need to talk with a vocational or personal counselor. At other times they may need to know the answers to questions like:

> How can I obtain unemployment?
> How can I get another job?
> Can I be retrained?

In these cases, you may need to find out the answers for them or guide them to the best resource to get the answers or help they need.

Remember: Low morale in this type of case is most often caused by a sense of helplessness or powerlessness. The best solution is to show that you care and help the employee take action.

Common Cause: Low Self-Esteem

Most people are unaware that one of the most common causes for problem behavior is low self-esteem.

WHAT IS SELF-ESTEEM?

"Self-esteem is appreciating one's own worth and importance, and having the character to be accountable for oneself and to act responsibly toward others."
— California State Task Force to Promote Self-Esteem
and Personal and Social Responsibility

Low self-esteem is often caused by focusing on the negative. Examples:

- I can't do . . .
- I'm not good at . . .
- My weaknesses are . . .
- I'm helpless at . . .

Whether the messages come from outside or inside the person, the negativity tears down self-esteem.

THE FOCUS OF OUR CULTURE

The stimulus and common cause for low self-esteem can be found in our culture.

Our school and business cultures are based in the critical thinking approach which looks for what is wrong in people and things. This negativity causes a negative view of oneself. People express their low self-esteem in many ways: from criticizing others, to seeking to dominate others, to withdrawing.

We mentioned earlier that new teammates listen the radio station WIIFM (What's In It For Me). People with low self-esteem listen to a different radio station — WAM! (Weaknesses Are Me). Victims listen to WEAM (Why's Everyone Against Me).

So what can you do?

To help boost your teammates' self-esteem, refer back to Skinner's philosophy of behavior modification: "Catch someone doing something right and give them positive reinforcement for that behavior." Continual, and justified, reinforcement for the desired behavior can help produce more of that same action. Additionally, notice and compliment the person for his/her traits and abilities. For example, "I really appreciate your ability to figure out how to fix the computer."

Helpful Questions

The following questions can be helpful to shift people's focus from their negatives to their strengths. You may want to use some of them during performance reviews, coaching sessions or other one-to-one meetings.

What do you consider your greatest work accomplishment?
What do you consider the most important contribution you make to our team?
What do you feel are your strengths?
How would your best friend describe you?
What would be the greatest compliment anyone could pay you?
What would you like most to be remembered for in your life?
Here is a suggestion to build confidence for a lifetime. At the end of each day, write down accomplishments, successes and joys.

How To Remove a Team Member

Occasionally team members cause more damage to the team than they make positive contributions. Sometimes even after the team has tried everything it can think of, the person still refuses to be a positive, contributing member. In these cases, it may be necessary to remove the person from the team. But how can he/she be removed without causing more damage to the team, and to its goals and projects? This is a sticky issue, with many areas of "It depends . . ."

Activity: If you had this situation, what would you do?
John is a member of your team. His behavior is characterized by:

- Criticizing everyone else's ideas.
- Monopolizing the conversations, and not listening to others.
- Not carrying through on his responsibilities, and always blaming others for his lack of timeliness.

John's skills and knowledge are important to the team, but his behavior has brought the team to a standstill and caused the team a great deal of emotional upheaval. John is unwilling to change his behavior. There are others who could take his place, but none have his level of knowledge. Politically, John is well connected within the organization.

Your challenge: Find a way to get John to leave or remove him from the team, so he does not harm what your team needs to do, nor harm the reputations of any team members. (Hint: He probably needs to "save face.") Be specific about what you would say and do.

* * * * *

The preceding is a good example for your team to consider during the training process. Having thought it through helps everyone realize the importance of positive team behavior.

Removing a team member can be a tough challenge. Or, it can simply be a part of each team member's assessment. Lesson #12: Assess Team Process Effectiveness shows you how to have periodic assessments that will make it self-evident, to both the problem person and the team, whenever anyone needs to leave the team. Using these assessment tools brings an objectivity to the removal and keeps the focus on the goal.

Lesson #12

Assess Team Process Effectiveness

★ Before Forming a Team
★ New or Problematic Teams
★ Once a Quarter

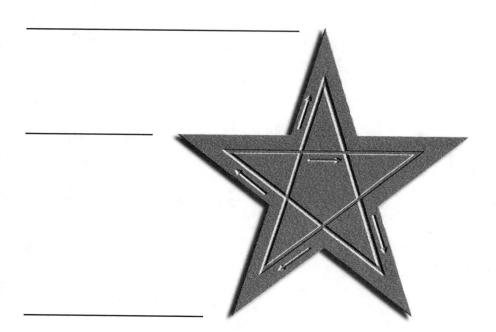

Stage III:
Implementing And Maintaining Star Teams[SM]

orking on a Star Team℠ requires a high level of understanding about yourself and your teammates. There are key times when it is important to take assessment of your skills, styles, interests, interactions and progress:

★ Before forming a team *(who should be on the team)*

★ At the first team meeting — of any new team *(personal styles and interests)*

★ New or problematic teams

★ Once every quarter *(overall processes, interrelationships and progress)*

Before Forming a Team

In order to assure the right people are on the team, a preliminary assessment is important. Ask these three questions.

PRE-TEAM PLANNING QUESTIONS

- What type of team do we need to accomplish this goal?
- What knowledge and vital characteristics are needed to work on this team to accomplish this goal?
- Who is available to commit the amount of time that this team needs?

When thinking about the characteristics needed, remember to consider their change style (Realist, Collaborator, Goal Seeker or Visionary). If you don't have one of the attributes that you need in any of the players, ask if any of the players can adapt or flex into that style while working with the team. As people become more experienced with working on different types of teams, they will hopefully learn how to flex into any of the styles needed.

By addressing these questions with the people invited to be on the team, members will be able to bypass some of the questions in the forming stage of team development. They will already know why they are on the team, and they should have a good idea of what others expect of them. We believe team membership should be voluntary. In consulting with companies who had mandated participation, we observed that the practice caused negativity which the team had to deal with, taking their focus from the goal.

Other important questions to ask about the goal, available resources and the power of the team were addressed earlier in this book.

AT THE FIRST TEAM MEETING

When a team is first forming, it is important that all members have a realistic perspective about themselves and how they work with others on a team. Time and angst can be minimized if the following questionnaire is completed by all team members and shared with the whole team.

Personal Preferences Survey

Instructions: Please complete this form with introspection and honesty. You will be sharing your responses with your teammates, so they will have a better understanding of how best to work with you. (There are no right or wrong answers.)

1. I prefer to work ❐ alone ❐ in a group

2. I prefer to work ❐ slowly ❐ quickly

3. I ❐ like ❐ do not like to compete

4. I prefer ❐ to lead ❐ to be led

5. I prefer to receive recognition (prioritize 1, 2, 3, 4):
   ____ one to one
   ____ in front of the team
   ____ with the team
   ____ in writing

6. What kind of work assignments, tasks and roles (Team Leader, Facilitator, Scribe, Timekeeper) really turn me on?

   _____

   _____

7. When people are giving me constructive feedback, what's important to me is

   _____

   _____

8. On this team, it is really important to me that

   _____

   _____

New or Problematic Teams

When a team is first organizing itself, the following Team Meeting Process Assessment can help members coalesce and improve their work together. We recommend the team take five to ten minutes at the end of each of their first few meetings to answer these questions. Once the team feels it is functioning well, it is still advisable to revisit these questions once a quarter.

These assessment questions are also useful for a team having problems with process or relationships. Ten to fifteen minutes at several consecutive meetings may need to be allocated to discuss them.

Team Meeting Process Assessment[1]

Instructions: Each person write your answers to each question, then discuss your responses with the entire group.

1. What did we do well in how we worked together today?

2. What specifically did we do that made it work for us?

3. Did we advance toward our goal? In what ways?

4. What do we want to do more of, less of or differently at our next meeting?

5. Did we follow the meeting guidelines? If not, what shall we do to improve next time?

Once a Quarter

At least once a quarter, longer term teams should go through the following two-part "Getting Even Better" overall assessment. It also can be used when the team feels there are some processing or relationship challenges and they need a way to analyze them. Any segment of this can be done with more frequency, depending on your need. We also recommend a new team experience this survey after four to five meetings if they are meeting on a weekly basis. You may want to cover the two parts at two different meetings.

Getting Even Better
Part 1: Team

Instructions: Consider how your team works together. Rate each of the following categories with a ranking of 1 to 5, ranging from 1(we don't have very much of that) to 5 (we are high in that).

____ Team member attendance at meetings is as expected

____ Members are clear on their process roles (Team Leader, Facilitator, Timekeeper, Scribe)

____ Members are clear on their task roles

____ We have the right people on the team

____ Agendas are helping us stay focused on the right subjects

____ Members are committed to the performance goals

____ Strategies for achieving goals are clear

____ Differences of opinion are handled with respect and logic

____ We are following our communication guidelines

____ We solve our problems well

____ Members enjoy working together

____ Members trust each other

____ Members carry through on their commitments between meetings

____ Executives are kept informed of the team's work

____ We have enough laughter

____ We are celebrating enough

____ We are on target to meet our goal(s)

____ The customer is benefitting by the work of our Star TeamSM

Part 2 is used to give and gather feedback on how each person has been as a team member. Two versions are shown, one for the member him/herself, and one for teammate feedback. Feel free to add or subtract any of the items, depending on what characteristics are needed for your team.

First each person completes a form about themselves, then one on each of the other team members. They can be completed outside of the meeting and delivered at a later team meeting. You can make them anonymous or signed. To help each person improve, we suggest that everyone look at the areas of improvement suggested by their colleagues. During a meeting, if any member is unclear about the feedback, he or she should ask for clarification or examples. Then each member should make a commitment to the team to work on the areas suggested — especially if more than one person suggested it. Additionally, each person can summarize a couple of things that were listed as strengths — especially if they were listed several times.

To set this up as a positive experience for everyone, approach it with the attitude that "We are all very good; we just want to be even better." Remember to share any verbal feedback with tact.

Getting Even Better
Part 2 — Personality

Instructions: Consider the characteristics below. Place an "S" beside those that best describe your Strengths in a team, and an "I" next to those that need Improvement. The more honest you are, the easier it will be to create good understanding and working relationships.

____ Cooperative	____ Volunteers to help others
____ Participative	____ Creative
____ Patient	____ Cope well with change
____ Organized	____ Open to try new things
____ Punctual	____ Resistant to change
____ Trustworthy	____ Follow through on commitments
____ Positive (approach issues constructively)	____ Fun to be with
____ Negative (tend to look for the problems, not the solutions)	____ Examine issues objectively
	____ Judge quickly
____ Open to others' ideas	____ Highly skilled in job/profession
____ Tactfully honest	____ High personal work standards
____ Aggressive (talk louder, more firmly than others to make your point)	____ Can be depended on
	____ Reluctant to move from own position or point of view
____ Assertive	____ Flexible in role, depending on what is needed
____ Easy to deal with	
____ Often involved in conflict	____ Make others feel good about themselves
____ The one who resolves conflict	
____ See others' points of view	____ Listen well
____ Willing to compromise	____ Interrupt others

Getting Even Better
Part 2 — Teammates

Teammate name _____

Instructions: Consider the characteristics below. Place an "S" beside those that best describe your teammate's Strengths in a team, and an "I" next to those that need Improvement.

____ Cooperative
____ Participative
____ Patient
____ Organized
____ Punctual
____ Trustworthy
____ Positive (approaches issues constructively)
____ Negative (tends to look for the problems, not the solutions)
____ Open to others' ideas
____ Tactfully honest
____ Aggressive (talk louder, more firmly than others to make your point)
____ Assertive
____ Easy to deal with
____ Often involved in conflict
____ The one who resolves conflict
____ Sees others' points of view
____ Willing to compromise

____ Volunteers to help others
____ Creative
____ Cope well with change
____ Open to try new things
____ Resistant to change
____ Follows through on commitments
____ Fun to be with
____ Examines issues objectively
____ Judges quickly
____ Highly skilled in job/profession
____ High personal work standards
____ Can be depended on
____ Reluctant to move from own position or point of view
____ Flexible in role, depending on what is needed
____ Makes others feel good about themselves
____ Listens well
____ Interrupts others

NOTES

1. Team Meeting Process Assessment adapted from the "Framework" technique developed by Enlightened Leadership International, Inc., of Englewood, CO, and described by the founders in: Ed Oakley and Doug Krug, *Enlightened Leadership: Getting to the Heart of Change* (New York: Simon and Schuster, 1991), 115-116.

Getting Results

Using teams effectively is a complex challenge, but when:

- A little forethought is used
- Management takes the time to establish a complete plan, involving some potential team members
- Everyone receives continual training to ease and speed growth
- Team members are willing to stretch to learn new skills
- Team members want to be a success
- Team members are willing to use self-discipline

. . . then teams can:

- Increase productivity!
- Create synergy!
- Raise motivation and participation!
- Increase spirit and enthusiasm!
- Reduce stress during tough challenges!
- Reach goals never attainable before!

A team is a time-proven tool for getting things done. Many lessons have been learned — often the hard way. By applying teams in new ways, in this new millennium, you can achieve stellar results — even in today's fast-changing environment.

"For decades great athletic teams have harbored one simple secret that only a few select business teams have discovered, and it is this: to play and win together, you must practice together."

— Lewis Edwards

Recommended Reading

Ashkenas, Ron and Dave Ulrich, Todd Jick and Steve Kerr, *The Boundaryless Organization*. San Francisco: Jossey-Bass Inc. Publishers, 1995.

Banks, Lydia, *Motivation in the Workplace: Inspiring Your Employees*. West Des Moines: American Media Publishing, 1997.

Capezio, Peter, *Supreme Teams: How to Make Teams Really Work*. National Press Publications, 1996.

Hackett, Donald and Charles L. Martin, *Facilitation Skills for Team Leaders*. Menlo Park: Crisp Publications, Inc., 1993.

Harshman, Carl and Steve Phillips, *Team Training: From Startup to High Performance*. New York: McGraw-Hill, Inc., 1996.

Hastings, Colin, Peter Bixby, and Rani Chaudhry-Lawton, *The Superteam Solution: Successful Teamworking in Organizations*. San Diego, CA: University Associates, Inc., 1987.

Hawkins, Charlie, *First Aid for Meetings: Quick Fixes and Major Repairs for Running Effective Meetings*. Wilsonville, OR: BookPartners, Inc., 1997.

Hendricks, Dr. William, *The Manager's Role As Coach*. Shawnee Mission, KS: National Press Publications, 1994.

Jerome, Paul J., *ReCreating Teams During Transition*. Irvine, CA: Richard Chang Associates, Inc., 1994.

Katzenbach, John R. and Douglas K. Smith, *The Wisdom of Teams* (Book on Tape). New York, NY: Harper Collins Publishing, Inc., 1994.

Klubnik, Joan P. and Penny Greenwood, *The Team-Based Problem Solver*. Burr Ridge, IL: Irwin Professional Publishing, Inc., 1994.

Lipnack, Jessica and Jeffrey Stamps, *Virtual Teams: Reaching Across Space, Time and Organizations with Technology*. New York: John Wiley & Sons, Inc., 1997.

Lloyd, Sam, *Leading Teams: The Skills for Success*. West Des Moines, IA: American Media Publishing, 1996.

Maddux, Robert B., *Team Building: An Exercise in Leadership*, revised edition. West Des Moines, IA: American Media Publishing, 1992.

Maginn, Michael D., *Effective Teamwork*. West Des Moines, IA: American Media Publishing, 1992.

Murphy, Jim, *Managing Conflict at Work*. West Des Moines, IA: American Media Publishing, 1994.

Nelson, Bob, *1001 Ways to Reward Employees*. New York: Workman Press, 1994.

Oakley, Ed and Krug, Doug, *Enlightened Leadership: Getting to the Heart of Change*. New York: Simon and Schuster, 1991.

Pokras, Sandy, *Team Problem Solving: Solving Problems Systematically*, revised edition. Menlo Park, CA: Crisp Publications, Inc., 1995.

Pokras, Sandy, *Working In Teams: A Team Member Guidebook*. Menlo Park, CA: Crisp Publications, Inc., 1997.

Wilson, Patricia, *Empowering the Self-Directed Team*. Shawnee Mission, KS: National Press Publications, 1993.

Resources

hen designing your rewards and motivation program, it is helpful to work with a company in the "specialty advertising" field to develop mementos or rewards that will be right for your needs. Following are two sources. The first is a national organization of specialty advertising professionals, which you can contact for local references, and the second is a proven, reputable specialty advertising firm which excels at customizing programs.

PROMOTIONAL PRODUCTS ASSOCIATION INTERNATIONAL

3125 Skyway Circle North
Irving, Texas 75038-3526
972-252-0404
Website: www.ppa.org

THE PALOMAR GROUP, INC.

6105 Puffer Road
Downers Grove, Illinois 60516
630-852-3324
E-mail: palomargrp@aol.com

About the Author

Janelle Brittain, MBA, CSP* is an internationally known consultant, trainer and speaker, who has nearly 30 years of business experience in training, sales, marketing and management. She has three other published books, a training film called "Flexible Thinking: Switching on Your Best," and several audio cassettes. In 1989, she left a successful career in high-tech sales to establish the Dynamic Performance Institute (DPI), whose mission is:

To help people be able to better handle their challenges of today and their unknown challenges of tomorrow. The tools and insights DPI offers will enable people to use more of their own faculties and inner resources, and to reduce stress and anguish while increasing the flow, meaning, and ability to get the results they want, in their life and life's work.

DPI has helped hundreds of companies and organizations build the skills of their people and establish processes that create an optimum environment for both the individual and the organization to grow. Janelle Brittain and her DPI team have created more than 100 hours of training programs on team building which are customized in programs for clients based on the results of their Teams Culture Alignment Assessment (TCAA). For your complementary TCAA, contact DPI at the address below.

Your Input Is Welcome

We continue to gather the lessons learned by companies and organizations who have implemented teams. To share your team building experiences so that others may benefit, please contact us at:

Dynamic Performance Institute

1542 W. Estes Avenue
Chicago, Illinois 60626
(Toll-free) 888-262-8686
Website: Dynamicperformance.com
E-mail: JanelleBri@aol.com

---

* CSP stands for Certified Speaking Professional, the highest earned award bestowed by the National Speakers Association. Only about 300 people worldwide have achieved this recognition.

Index

I

IBM, 50, 61
individualistic approach
    and efficiency, 21
    and significant stakeholders, 21–22
    and time crunches, 21
    and unique decisions, 20
Industrial Age, 7, 8, 17, 25
Information Age, 8, 55
Intergalactic Digital Research, 61

J

James, Richard, 136
Johns, Steve, 26
Jordan, Michael, 120

K

Kaizen, 8
Knowledge Age, 8, 51, 55, 129, 130
K Shoes, 19
Krug, Doug, 110

L

Lauterbach, Nancy, 124
low morale, due to changes, 188–90

M

managers. *See also* teams
    and coaching, 109–12
        feedback procedures, 110–11
        performance consultant, 112–14
        performance delivery keys, 114–16
        Performance Training Preparation Template, 114
    and leadership, 107–8
    roles, 105–7
Massachusetts Institute of Technology, 20
Meetings Manager, The, 134
Mell, Darrell, 129
Meyrowitz, Joshua, 58, 60
Microsoft, 61
Milwaukee Mutual Insurance, 19
Motorola, ix, 126, 135–36

N

No Sense of Place, 58, 60